SHIRE GARDEN HISTORY

Florists' Flowers
and Societies

Ruth Duthie

Printed in Great Britain by C. I. Thomas & Sons (Haverfordwest) Ltd, Press Buildings, Merlins Bridge, Haverfordwest, Dyfed SA61 1XF.

British Library Cataloguing in Publication Data available.

In memory of E. S. D. and R. C. P.

(Cover photograph) Spray of mixed flowers on a marble ledge. Thomas Robins (the Elder), 1768. All the florists' flowers are shown except the pink and carnation, which bloom later in the year. (Fitzwilliam Museum, Cambridge.)

(Title page photograph) A vase of flowers of 1641 in Matthew Merian, 'Florilegium Renovatum'. Tulips, single hyacinths, carnations, anemones and daffodils are shown but not auriculas or ranunculuses. (Courtesy of the Royal Horticultural Society.)

(Below) Eighteenth-century caricature: the entomologist trampling over the florist's tulips. (Courtesy of Mr P. H. Goodchild.)

14691

2883307   DUTHIE, R.   Florists'
                         Flowers and
         MB 9/88   Societies
                           3.48

C/

635
9
DUT

Please renew/return this item by the last date shown.

So that your telephone call is charged at local rate,
please call the numbers as set out below:

	From Area codes 01923 or 0208:	From the rest of Herts:
Renewals:	01923 471373	01438 737373
Enquiries:	01923 471333	01438 737333
Minicom:	01923 471599	01438 737599

L32b

PLA

MB

Contents

Acknowledgements
Warmest thanks are due to Dr John Harvey for his help over the years; to Rosemary Verey for the use of her fine library; to Dr Brent Elliott of the Lindley Library (Royal Horticultural Society) for his advice and to all those named who have supplied photographs; to Mavis Batey, Sylvia Landsberg, Katharine Johnstone and Gordon Rowley. Amongst my florist friends thanks to John Barlow, Hubert Calvert, David Hastings, Frank Jacques, Jack Wemyss-Cooke and Audrey Robinson. Photographs are by the author unless otherwise stated.

4

1. *Scattered flowers on the margins of a page of a Flemish Book of Hours, about 1500. (Courtesy of the Trustees of Sir John Soane's Museum.)*

Who were the florists?

Today the word 'florist' is used of someone who keeps a shop where cut flowers and pot plants are sold. However, that was not its original meaning. It was first applied to a person who grew plants for the sake of their decorative flowers rather than for any useful property the plant might have. Later it came to refer to one who grew only certain kinds of flowering plants and these to a very high standard, their excellence being tested at competitions held with fellow florists. It was only towards the end of the nineteenth century that the word came to have its modern meaning.

Even before any effort was made to improve flowering plants by cultivation, people took pleasure in flowers and used them in their art, often giving them religious significance. In medieval Europe the exquisitely illustrated devotional 'Books of Hours' have the margins of the pages decorated with naturalistic drawings of scattered flowers. Similar representations of flowers appear in the tapestries of the period. Though these plants could have been grown in the monastery garden they were essentially wild flowers.

Plants were of supreme importance to another group: the herbalists. Though herbs were required for many purposes in the household, as food and in tasks like dyeing or making cosmetics, their study was mainly confined to those concerned with medicine. Greek physicians had laid down the basis of treatment but the original herbals had perished and the drawings of plants had been copied and recopied so often without recourse to examining living specimens that they had lost their usefulness for identification. It was of little value knowing the properties of a plant if it could not be recognised when growing.

In keeping with the spirit of the renaissance, by early in the sixteenth century herbalists were once more collecting plants, naming and making accurate drawings of them. With the advent of the printed book illustrated by woodcuts the information they had gained became widely available. Some of the most beautifully illustrated herbals belong to this period: those of Otto Brunfels (1530) and of Leonard Fuchs (1543). In the middle of the sixteenth century a sixth-century illustrated copy of the Herbal of Dioscorides was discovered in Constantinople by Ogier de Busbecq, the ambassador from the Holy Roman Emperor to the Sultan, Suleiman the Magnificent. Not only did de Busbecq

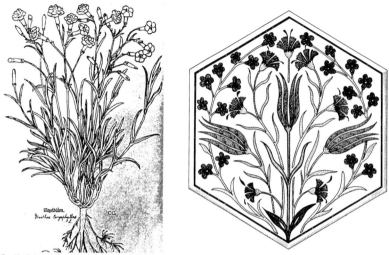

2 (left). *Dianthus from Leonard Fuchs' 'De Historia Stirpium', 1542.*
3 (right). *Tulip, hyacinth and carnation as they might appear on an Iznik ware plate of 1550-1650, showing the form of flower admired in the Ottoman Empire. (Drawing by Laura Potter.)*

recognise this volume for what it was but he also sent to Vienna a number of plants which he saw growing in Turkish gardens and which were new to western Europe. By 1569 this great herbal was at the imperial court of Vienna (where it can still be seen in the National Library); herbalists could compare the plants they found with its illustrations, for Dioscorides had always been considered one of the greatest of Greek authorities.

By the mid sixteenth century herbalists were not only examining living plants but were making collections of them from specific areas, as was done by Charles de l'Ecluse in Spain and later in the Alps. This man, usually known by the Latin form of his name, Clusius, was a Fleming by birth but was a refugee in this period of religious persecution. He is now looked on as the father of the Dutch bulb industry but can also be called a founder of botany, a science then becoming a study distinct from herbalism. Clusius and other investigators were becoming interested in plants for their own sakes and were attempting, although not yet very successfully, to classify them. Plants were then named for their supposed properties so a *Primula* could be called *Sanicula* referring to its ability to heal wounds, or *Paralytica* because of 'his virtues in curing palsies, cramps and convulsions'.

Towards the end of the century the great publishing house of Plantin was established at Antwerp. A great collection of plant drawings was made there; though not as beautiful as the engravings of the older German herbals, their accuracy and convenient size made them valuable and they continued to be used for a long time, appearing in books by many different writers.

These Plantin books included illustrations of plants newly introduced from East and West. From the Americas came plants primarily from the wild, such as sunflowers, 'African' marigolds and Marvel of Peru (*Mirabilis jalapa*), as well as maize and potato. The introductions from the east were mainly cultivated plants from Turkish gardens. The gardens of the Ottoman Empire were far finer than those of contemporary Europe and there was also a cult of certain plants, particularly the rose, carnation, hyacinth, narcissus and, above all, the tulip. Gardeners selected plants with particularly fine flowers and bred from them. The qualities admired by these gardeners differed from those later favoured by European growers and the slender, graceful forms of their plants were represented in the Turkish art of the sixteenth and seventeenth centuries. De Busbecq sent plants from Ottoman gardens to Vienna but they were also reaching Western cities, like Venice, in the course of trade and both from gardens and from the wild. These Eastern plants included tulips, hyacinths, ranunculuses, crown imperials and anemones, as well as the shrubs Clusius is known to have sent, lilac and philadelphus.

From the 1540s universities began to establish botanic gardens, then called physic gardens. The first were at Padua and Pisa and other Italian towns; these were followed by those of German and French cities and that of Leyden in Holland. The first English botanic garden was established at Oxford in 1621. In these gardens the fullest possible range of plants was grown but private gardens were also being created and in these some selection could be practised, with plants being chosen for their aesthetic qualities and planted so as to enhance their beauty. Certain plants, chosen for special features, were used for breeding and of their seedlings only the finest were kept. Hybridisation was not practised since the sexuality of plants was not then understood, but accidental crosses between related species and between garden varieties must have taken place.

Good new varieties could not be increased by seed, for seedlings do not breed true, so some form of vegetative propagation had to be practised: the art of grafting of fruit trees had long been known and herbaceous plants could be increased by some form of splitting, such as by taking cuttings or using the bulbs or other underground parts which the plant could make.

In modern usage a garden variety showing a desirable quality is called a cultivar, whereas a wild plant having an unusual feature is known as a variety. The production and the naming of cultivars tells us much about the relative degrees of improvement in plants over a period of time. At first, when there are only a few new kinds, they are given descriptive names, such as 'Tradescant's great rose daffodil' ('rose' because it was double) or the auricula 'Mistress Buggs her fine purple'. However, once a large number of cultivars had been produced, often showing only minor differences, this became impossible and so purely arbitrary names were given, such as 'Semper Augustus' and 'Viceroy', the two most expensive tulips of the Dutch tulipomania of the 1630s, or the carnations 'Nymph Royal' and 'General Wiggons'. John Parkinson, whose *Paradisi in Sole, Paradisus Terrestris* (in future referred to as *Paradisus*) appeared in 1629, used such arbitrary cultivar names only for carnations, such as 'Crystall' and those mentioned above. However, when in 1676 the second edition of John Rea's *Flora, seu de Florum cultura* (in future, *Flora*) was published he named more than 360 carnations, about 200 tulips, 120 poppy anemones and 25 ranunculuses. Although he was fond of auriculas and had raised some new ones himself, he used descriptive names such as 'Mistress Buggs her fine purple' or 'black imperial'.

Thus, by the mid seventeenth century four plants (carnation, tulip, anemone and ranunculus) were in a special category and later these, with some additions, became known as 'florists' flowers'. The word florist is believed to have been used first in 1623, when Sir Henry Wotton wrote of having made 'acquaintance with some excellent florists (as they are stiled)' and Parkinson used the term a number of times in 1629. The only restriction on what the florist grew was that his plants were selected for beauty rather than for utility. Towards the end of the century, a degree of specialisation can be perceived when Samuel Gilbert, Rea's son-in-law, wrote in his *Florists Vade-Mecum* of 1682 about 'the trifles adored amongst countrywomen but of no esteem to a Florist who is taken up with things of more value': yet amongst these trifles were a number of plants which are still grown in our gardens, such as hollyhocks and Canterbury bells. Nevertheless Gilbert did not suggest that the florist's flowers be restricted to carnation, tulip, anemone, ranunculus and, his own favourite, the auricula, even if these plants already formed a special group. It was only towards the middle of the next century that these, with the hyacinth, polyanthus and, much later, the pink, were so regarded. These eight formed the classic florists' flowers and remained exclusively so until the pansy and dahlia joined them in the 1830s.

A change in outlook took place in the middle of the nineteenth century, when many more plants began to be referred to as florists' flowers (in fact, any plant for which separate classes were provided at horticultural shows), so chrysanthemums and hollyhocks, as well as bedding plants like pelargoniums and calceolarias, were included. Even woody plants like roses, camellias and fuchsias were called florists' flowers.

The modern use of 'florist' as one who retails cut flowers developed around the 1870s. J. C. Loudon, writing in 1822, explained that there were then two kinds of florists: one the kind described, who grew his fine flowers and competed with fellow florists, and the other sort, whom he called the market-florist. The latter grew flowers to sell as nosegays and pots of flowering plants and other ornamentals, such as palms, which were sold or rented to decorate houses on special occasions. Gradually these formal displays of potted plants gave way to arrangements in vases of cut flowers. Then, as more and more people began to buy such flowers, the role of the market-florist changed. During the same period the importance of the old-time florist diminished as fewer of his kind of shows were held, so the need to qualify the market-florist disappeared, and he became known simply as a florist.

Returning to the seventeenth century, very soon after the introduction of the word florist, we hear of florists forming groups with like-minded people to meet and hold feasts. Best known is the society of florists in Norwich, already in existence in 1631, but a society must also have existed soon afterwards in London, for when the nurseryman William Lucas of Strand Bridge made his will in 1677 he bequeathed the cost of a gold ring to every member of the 'Society or Clubb of Florist'.

In addition to the botanical and vernacular names for plants there were many colloquial ones, such as bears ears (for auriculas) or paigle (for cowslip) or the vast number for the wild pansy, *Viola tricolor,* of which heartsease is only the commonest. Parkinson provided many colloquial names for the abnormal forms of primrose and cowslip, then so much loved. Jackanapes-

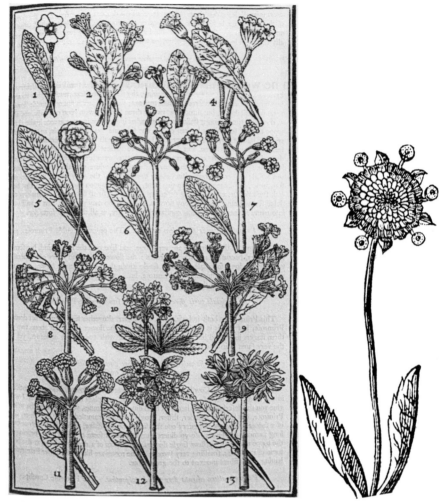

4 (left). *Primroses and cowslips from John Parkinson's 'Paradisus', 1629.*
5 (right). *Parkinson's 'hen-and-chickens' daisy.*

on-horseback, he used of one where the green calyx was enlarged
to form a kind of ruff round the coloured corolla (what we now
usually call a Jack-in-the-green), but he also used it for what is
now called a 'hen-and-chickens' daisy, in which a number of small
daisies form from the lower side of the first-formed flower.

Parkinson illustrated further abnormal primulas and other plants.

In those early days of gardening, when newly introduced plants were unobtainable or very costly to buy, it is easy to see how welcome such oddities would have been to those wanting some variety in their gardens. They would not, however, have appealed to the florist, though he would have welcomed other teratological plants, such as those with double flowers: in these the pollen-bearing stamens and sometimes also the seed-bearing carpels became petalloid.

Again, he would have liked the appearance of some variegation in the colour of the flower, giving him the striped and speckled gilliflower (carnation) or tulip. Such features were fastened upon by the florist and plants showing them were selected for breeding and new cultivars produced. As time passed the taste of the florist changed: for instance, the double-flowered auricula so admired in the seventeenth century went out of fashion in the eighteenth, only to be revived (to the horror of some!) in very recent years.

Unusual plants could have been collected from the countryside and improved ones exchanged at florists' meetings but by quite early in the seventeenth century nurseries had been established, mainly in or near London, where both seeds and plants could be bought. Catalogues from a few of them have survived, a particularly full one from the William Lucas who left the gold rings to his fellow members. Another of these early nurserymen was Ralph Tuggie of Westminster, who died in 1632 and was highly praised by Parkinson, especially for his carnations and auriculas. His nursery was continued by his son, Richard. The John Tradescants, father and son, had a nursery of repute at Lambeth and again catalogues of the plants they grew exist; their collection of fruit trees was notable. George Ricketts of Hoxton also offered fine fruit trees and sent a price list to Sir Thomas Hanmer of Bettisfield in North Wales, whom he provided with anemones, carnations and auriculas. Outside the metropolis nurseries existed at York and Oxford in the seventeenth century, while John Rea and, after him, Samuel Gilbert had a nursery, though maybe of a limited kind, at the remote village of Kinlet in Shropshire. Rea provided Hanmer with plants and certainly with fruit trees, while Samuel Gilbert provided a list of auriculas which he said was 'for an advertisement'.

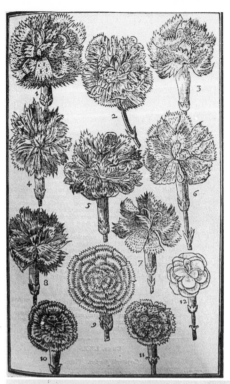

6. Some of Parkinson's carnations and gilliflowers, including 'Crystall' (5), 'granpere' (7) and 'Master Tuggie his Rose Gilliflower' (12).

7. From a book believed to have been a Belgian work. Upper left there are pots of auriculas on a stage. ('Hortus Belgicus', 1962. Copyright of Bibliothèque Royal Albert 1er, Brussels.)

NOUVEAU
TRAITÉ
DE LA
CULTURE PARFAITE
DES
OREILLES D'OURS
OU
AURICULES.

A PARIS,
Et se vend
A BRUSSELLES,
Chez GILLES STRYCKWANT,
ruë de Berg-straet.

M. D. CC. XXXVIII.

Florists' societies and feasts in the seventeenth and eighteenth centuries

It is frequently suggested that the custom of forming florists' societies was introduced into England by the Flemish refugees who settled here in the sixteenth century, particularly when the persecution was at its height during the governership of the Duke of Alba (1567-73). However, there is no evidence that such societies of flower lovers existed in the Low Countries at such an early date, nor is it at all probable that the Flemings could have brought auriculas or other florists' flowers with them. What can be said is that some of these refugees did improve English market-gardening by the introduction of new kinds of vegetables and by better methods of cultivation.

Our knowledge of the florists' society of seventeenth-century Norwich comes from a play and two poems written to celebrate their feasts. The play, *Rhodon and Iris,* by Ralph Knevet, was referred to as a 'Pastoral as it was presented at a Florist Feast at Norwich 3 May 1631'. The preface was addressed to the author's 'much respected friends, the Society of Florists' and it is clear that some of the members were connected with the commerce of the city. There is no indication that any flowers were exhibited and it may have been a purely social gathering for the flower lovers and gardeners of the town. Both the poems refer to this social aspect and one (Mathew Stevenson's) has the line 'Let chearly cups crown a carowsing day', while both mention the disapproval shown by local puritans at the holding of a feast to Flora.

William Stroud's poem is called 'A Prologue crown'd with Flowers, On the Florists Feast at Norwich'. It can be dated to the years 1632-5 since Stroud was chaplain to Bishop Richard Corbet, who held the see of Norwich only for those years. This poem, though it refers to some flowers, including the then very popular tulip, does not suggest there was any floral display. It is filled with delight at the beauties of nature, as in the lines:

The Springs Returne, the Earths new Livery
Inheaven'd with aemulous light of starry Flowres.
The woodes shrill Chanters singing short the howres.

Mathew Stevenson was the author of the other poem, 'At the Florists Feast at Norwich. Flora wearing a Crown', which was published in 1645. Many of the lines contain names, all in italics, such as '*Crystall*', 'both *Wiggons*', '*gray Halo*', '*Appelles*' and '*Nymph Royall*'. These, at first incomprehensible, turn out to be the names of carnations, many of which appeared in the long list given by John Rea in 1676, particularly amongst those he regarded as old-fashioned. They were also amongst those illustrated by Parkinson and Alexander Marshal (figures 6 and 66). Such florists' feasts must have continued to be held at Norwich, for a reference was made to them by the Cambridge botanist John Ray towards the end of the century.

Though there is no evidence for the existence of societies of flower-lovers in the Low Countries in the sixteenth century, some were formed in the seventeenth century, though of a limited kind and unlike those in England. Henry van Oosten ('the Leyden gardener') in the *Dutch Gardner* of 1703 described the formation of a society in the Netherlands to regulate the Dutch tulip trade as the bubble of tulipomania burst in 1637. He also wrote of the formation the same year of the Flemish society dedicated to St Dorothy, the patron saint of flower-lovers, whose members, also tulip fanciers, met to hold 'sweet Conversation and pleasant Consortship'. Such St Dorothy societies continued to exist in Flanders and between 1648 and 1651 were established in Brussels, Ghent and Bruges. The record of the Bruges society shows it was limited to eighteen persons, all members of the higher clergy and wealthy landowners, who met on the saint's day, 6 February, to celebrate Mass and hold a banquet. Even in the 1730s there were similarly named societies in towns of what is now known as Belgium and in northern France, but for auricula, not tulip, lovers. These societies were described by the author of the *Noveau Traité de la culture parfaite des Oreilles d'Ours ou Auricules* (1738) (figure 7), who was probably an abbé of Amiens. Many, though not all, of these auricula growers were connected with the Church.

By the beginning of the eighteenth century information about meetings of English florists is found in some local newspapers. As early as 1707 the *Norwich Gazette* of 5 July had the following advertisement. 'The Florists Feast, or Entertainment for lovers of Flowers and Gardens will be kept at Mr Thomas Riggs in St Swithin's Lane on Tuesday the 8th day of July next. Tickets will be had at 2s 6d each at the aforesaid Mr Thomas Riggs.'

Advertisements continued to appear for such meetings in Norwich and also in Kings Lynn. Early in the century annual feasts were also being held by a 'Royal Society of Gardiners' at York. As figure 8 shows, the copper plate used to summon their members carried the arms of Queen Anne (1702-14). In 1738 an advertisement appeared in the *York Courant* offering a gold ring

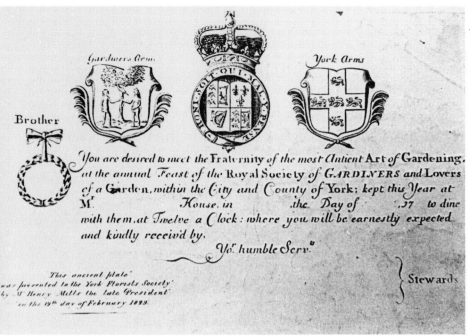

Gardiners Arms

York Arms

Brother

You are desired to meet the Fraternity of the most Antient Art of Gardening, at the annual Feast of the Royal Society of GARDINERS and Lovers of a Garden, within the City and County of York; kept this Year at Mr. House, in the Day of 17 to dine with them at Twelve a Clock: where you will be earnestly expected and kindly received by.

Yo.r humble Serv.t

This ancient plate was presented to the York Florists Society by Mr Henry Mills the late President on the 19th day of February 1829.

Stewards

8. *A copper plate dating from the reign of Queen Anne and presented to the Ancient Society of York Florists in 1829. (Photograph: Mr and Mrs K. W. Booth.)*

to the person who showed 'the best blown Carnation' at the feast. (To 'blow' meant 'to bloom' or 'to be in flower'.) Because of their small size, newspapers at this time carried little local news, so most of the information about feasts comes from advertisements. Happily the *Craftsman* of 16th April 1729 was an exception and reports on an unusually well-attended feast. 'On Tuesday last a great Feast of Gardiners call'd Florists was held in the Dog in Richmond Hill, at which were present about 130 in Number; after Dinner several shew'd their Flowers (most of them Auricula's) and five ancient and judicious Gardiners were Judges to determine whose flowers excelled ... a Gardiner of Barnes in Surrey was so well furnished with good Flowers, that the Judge in the affair, ordered him two Spoons and one Ladle.' Silver spoons were the usual prize but to receive two and a ladle was outstanding.

By the mid eighteenth century there were weekly newspapers covering the areas around Worcester, Gloucester, Ipswich, Newcastle upon Tyne and Canterbury, as well as York and Norwich. Advertisements for florists' feasts are found in all of them. The auricula was the flower exhibited at spring, and the carnation at summer, feasts. By the second half of the century many more towns had local publications and it is evident that florists' societies had been formed throughout the country, apart from the South-west (as no reports have been found of feasts being held south and west of Trowbridge). These gatherings were almost invariably held in public houses, the flowers being given to the stewards by midday, while the dinner, usually referred to as 'the good ordinary', took place at 1 p.m., after which the flowers, having been judged, were passed round the table. The flowers could be shown either growing in pots or 'cropt'. Figure 9 shows what an eighteenth-century feast might have been like, though this engraving was newly executed for the *Florist* of 1851. Auriculas and carnations continued to give their names to the feast but polyanthuses and often hyacinths were also exhibited and given prizes at the spring meetings. Only in Suffolk were there notices of tulip shows. Feasts were at their height in the 1770s and on into the 1780s. For instance, *Jackson's Oxford Journal* of 25th July 1772 carried three advertisements for feasts, printed one above the other.

At first only a few prizes were awarded but, as time went on, the number was increased by subdivision of the shows into separate types of plants. This was first reported at carnation feasts, when at Nottingham in 1775 separate prizes were offered for 'bezar, flake and pickatee carnations'. Soon first, second and third prizes were being awarded for each class, as well as a prize for the finest seedling. The naming of the winning seedling was an important ceremony during the afternoon. Though the prize was usually a large silver spoon, it could also be plate to a certain value or even cash. When the value was mentioned it could be as much as £2, the second prize about half that value and the prizes for third place and for the best seedling 5 shillings. The most useful indication of how generous the prizes were lies in the present value of a solid silver tablespoon, such as was so commonly given as first prize. At a florists' show at Atherton in the Midlands in 1791 twelve prizes were being offered at a total cost of £8 11s 0d.

In the *Ipswich Journal* of 1786 a show was advertised to take place at Woodbridge on 8th May and was duly reported as follows. 'Monday last, being the annual show of Auriculas, the gentlemen florists and their friends met at the Bull in this town, when after partaking of an elegant dinner, three gentlemen from Ipswich were chosen umpires to discuss the merits of the prize flowers, when after three-quarters of an hour inspection, a flower called 'Ardent's Empress of Russia' of 14 pips, was bought in as

9. Engraving of 'Florists of Olden Times', newly made for the 'Florist', 1851. (Courtesy of Mrs Rosemary Verey.)

the best flower, the property of Mr Henry Winson [pips are the individual flowers of the 'truss' of an auricula or polyanthus]; another of the same name containing 12 pips, as second best, the property of Mr John Calver, both of this place; a seedling of 4 pips, raised by the first gentlemen, was entitled to the last prize ... After the show, the seedling was named 'Winson's Dutchess of Devonshire'. The ceremony over, the three flowers were placed on the table surrounded by the company, who regaled themselves 'till ten o'clock, when they retired well satisfied with the productions of the day.' Henry Winson, the prize-winner, must have been a successful raiser of auriculas, for his varieties, including one called 'Woodbridge', appear in many of the catalogues of the period. Figure 11 illustrates a striped auricula called 'Empress of Russia' but it cannot be proved for certain that this was Arden's (not Ardent), for a nurseryman called Gorton had also called one of his auriculas 'Empress of Russia'; both varieties were listed in many catalogues of the period.

In the 1770s the *Bristol Journal* reported some local feasts, at one of which the auricula 'Vice's Green Seedling' gained first and second prize. This cultivar (known to have been one of the earliest with edged flowers) and 'Severn's Fame', which won first prize in the next year, also figure in catalogues. This second variety was exhibited by Mr Sixsmith, gardener to Gabriel Goldney, the owner of the fine Clifton garden with its famous grotto. It is rare to have information about the employment of

FLORIST's FEAST.

ON Tuesday the 4th of August next, a FLO-
RIST's FEAST will be held at the House of Richard Wall, at the SHIP Inn, in OXFORD ; where,
for the Encouragement of Industry and Care, the foll-w-
ing Prizes will be given, viz.

To him that shews the fix beft and compleatest whole-
blown CARNATIONS, of different Sorts, a large Silver
Spoon.

To him that shews the fix second beft and compleatest
whole-blown CARNATIONS, of different Sorts, Five
Shillings.

To him that shews the beft Seedling CARNATION,
Two Shillings and Six pence.

The Flowers to be delivered into the Care of the
Stewards, before Dinner is on the Table, which will be
precisely at Two o'Clock. No Perfon is entitled to shew,
unless he takes a Ticket. All Tickets not difperfed of,
are desired to be return'd on Friday before the Feaft.

                Richard Williams, }
                W. Fortie, jun.   } STEWARDS.

A FLORIST's FEAST

WILL be held at Mr. Clark's, at the SWAN
Inn, in BICESTER, on Monday the 10th of
August next, where the Company of all Gentlemen,
Florifts, Gardeners, &c. will be accepted ; at which
Place there will be a shew of CARNATIONS. And for
the Encouragement of Industry and Care, the three fol-
lowing Prizes will be given, viz.

For the faireft and compleatest whole-blowing Carnation, of fix different Sorts, a large Silver Spoon.

For the fix second-beft, of fix different Sorts, Five
Shillings.   And

For the beft Seedling Carnation, Half a Crown.

                STEWARDS.
Mr. Clarey, Steeple Afton. | Mr. Howlett, Bicefter,
Mr. Pullus, ——— Heath, | Mr. Crook, Brill, &c s,
Mr. Jaurfon, Merton. | Mr. Robarts, Eanbury.
Mr. Richards, Adderbury, |

A FLORIST's FEAST

WILL be held at Mr. ROBERTS's, the
QUEEN's HEAD, in BANBURY, OXFORD-
SHIRE, on Monday the 3d of August next ; where, for
the Encouragement of Industry and Care, the following
Prizes will be given, viz.

For the fix beft and compleatest whole-blown CAR-
NATIONS, of different Sorts, a Prize of a large Silver
Spoon.

For the fix second-beft, Five Shillings.

And for the beft Seedling Carnation, Half a Crown.

                STEWARDS.
Mr. Clifcut, Banbury, | Mr. Clary, Afton,
Mr. Haywa d, Banbury, | Mr. Richards, Aldetbury,
Mr. Mumford Aftrup, | Mr. Sharrog, Mariton,
Mr. Clarke, Bicefter, | Mr. Dixon, Edgcott.

10 (left). *Advertisements for three florists' feasts in Jackson's 'Oxford Journal',
25th July 1772. (Courtesy of Oxford County Libraries.)*
11 (right). *The auricula 'Empress of Russia'. (Private collection. Supplied by
Sothebys by kind permission of the owner.)*

florists; Adam Sixsmith is the only gentleman's gardener known
to have attended florists' meetings.

Pink feasts were advertised towards the end of the eighteenth
century for it was only then that the flower was regarded as
sufficiently improved to be acceptable as a florists' flower. Mary
Mitford wrote in *Our Village* (1826) of a retired innkeeper who
'lent his willing aid ... at pink feasts and melon feasts'. Melons
also figured at shows, generally at those held for carnations.
Melons required the protection of a hot-bed for their ripening
and so were grown by the better-off, unlike the gooseberry,

which also became a competition fruit towards the end of the eighteenth century, and which was grown mainly by artisans, prizes being given for the heaviest berry. Gooseberry shows were held most widely in industrial areas, and indeed a few still take place in Cheshire and at Egton Bridge in Yorkshire.

Newspaper accounts tell little of the societies which organised the shows. It seems clear that most of the business was conducted after dinner, when stewards were elected and plans made for the following year's show. More is known about those few societies whose records have survived. The earliest of these (though the least characteristic) was the Dublin Florists' Club. Its minute book for the years 1746-66 is preserved by the Royal Irish Academy. This Irish society shared some of the features of that of Bruges since its membership was confined to thirty, all landed gentry or military officers. Members met monthly to dine and drink innumerable toasts, including one to the auricula in the first half of the year and to the carnation in the second. The society also gave encouragement to Irish nurserymen by offering prizes for the finest auricula, polyanthus, ranunculus and carnation raised.

In 1768 the Ancient Society of York Florists was formed; this very well documented society is still in existence and holds three shows annually, the two autumn ones chiefly for dahlias and chrysanthemums. The records, more than mere minute books, are preserved in York Central Library and give information about the membership, accounts, shows, the names of successful exhibitors and the flowers that won the prizes. A full set of rules was drawn up and for the first seventy years the feast was held on the day of the auricula show, at which the polyanthus and hyacinth were also exhibited; the tulip show followed in May, that for the ranunculus in June and for the carnation in August. Pink shows were added at the beginning of the nineteenth century and for a few years there was a class for anemones at the tulip show. The society remained faithful to these classic florists' flowers for a long period, though dahlias became popular after 1840; classes for pansies and for a few other kinds of plants were added around the middle of the century. After 1840 the annual feast was held on the day of the dahlia show.

Another society which began life in the eighteenth century and is still in existence is the Paisley Florist Society. It was founded in 1782 and its records are kept at the Museum and Art Gallery at Paisley in Scotland. Members of this society met weekly during the flowering season and, though the eight florists' kinds were the

12. *Snuff mull presented to Mr Archibald Duncan for the twelve best pinks on 2nd July 1813 by the Paisley Florist Society. (Photograph: Mr J. M. Forrester.)*

competition flowers, border plants were not neglected. Members still meet nine times a year and hold an annual show. Horticultural literature makes much mention of 'Paisley pinks'.

One of the few horticultural writers of the eighteenth century to describe florists' societies was the Reverend William Hanbury of Church Langton in Leicestershire. In a long section on 'Prize Flowers' in his two-volume book, *The Whole Body of Planting and Gardening* (1770-1), he wrote of how widely florists clubs had been formed and that 'feasts are now become general, and are regularly held at towns, at proper distances, almost all over England'. Furthermore, he stated that weavers were already winning prizes at these feasts. These weavers were of course handloom workers based at home and, as Hanbury pointed out, they could easily leave their work to move their special plants into favourable positions as weather conditions dictated.

Hanbury, who was well aware of the landscape movement (then at its height), made it clear how suited were florists' kinds of plants to those with small town gardens. It is evident that many members of the York society were tradesmen, often apothecaries, since they would have had gardens for medicinal herbs. Nurserymen, in whom York was rich, were also active in the society and the first two secretaries, who kept records for more than fifty years, were writing masters. Though some of the local gentry were among the early members, there is no evidence of their taking an active part in the running of the society. In Paisley it is clear that skilled weavers played an important part in the society, while in Nottingham and Leicester some members were framework knitters but tradesmen were also active.

It is clear from the frequent mention of prizes being given for the best seedlings that florists were raising their own cultivars and both seed and plants could be exchanged at their meetings, but there were also many nurseries, some specialising in florists' varieties. The number of cultivars almost defies belief. Volume four of Richard Weston's *The Universal Botanist and Nurseryman*(1777) lists the auriculas, polyanthuses and carnations obtainable from James Maddock of Walworth, London. Of the 310 auriculas the most expensive cost £2 2s 0d; none cost less than 1 shilling. Of the cultivars mentioned both 'Severn's Fame' and 'Vice's Green Seedling' cost 2 shillings, which suggests that they were fairly old varieties, since the price fell as they became more widely available. The 54 polyanthuses were not priced and 48 of Mattock's own seedlings were also named. The name of the raiser and the price were given for the two hundred carnations; none was as costly as the more expensive auriculas but the average price was about the same. No pinks were mentioned in this catalogue of the 1770s.

The other plants listed were imported from 'the most esteemed and curious Dutch Florists' and were obtainable from English nurserymen. No less than 1100 ranunculuses were named and briefly described; they varied in price from just under £1 for special kinds but most were far less and were sold at so much the hundred. The 804 tulips were divided into groups according to colour and time of flowering; the finest kind of bulb cost over £2 but the average was about 2 shillings. The 575 hyacinths were also divided into groups depending on colour and whether single- or double-flowered. At this date hyacinth bulbs were more expensive than those of tulips: one called 'Black Flora' cost £21 and a few others almost as much but the popular old variety 'Koning van Groote Brittanje' (figure 43) was by then less than 2 shillings. 108 anemones were also named and described; they were the least expensive of these 'roots'. Crocuses, daffodils and some other bulbous plants also figured in these lists.

A number of other catalogues have survived from the end of the eighteenth century and agree well with Maddock's in the varieties named and in their prices. As well as general nurseries there were some which specialised in certain florists' plants: such was Thomas Biggs of Salisbury which in 1782 stocked over 250 auriculas. Both forms of 'Empress of Russia' were available but he gave no prices since he said these varied from year to year. His catalogue was not issued yearly. Nurseries throughout the country stocked a great many similarly named cultivars, thereby demonstrating a nationwide distribution.

In spite of the addition of pink shows, the number of advertisements for florists' meetings decreased markedly from the 1790s. One suggested reason for this decline was that economic conditions during the Napoleonic Wars made growing and showing these plants more difficult. Another is that by the end of the century the feasts had fallen into ill repute, having become little more than drinking parties. Undoubtedly they must have been convivial occasions for the 1786 feast at Woodbridge did not break up until 10 p.m. which must have been long after all the business of the day had been concluded. Thomas Hogg, in his book *A concise and practical Treatise on the Carnation etc.* (1822) supports the suggestion of florists' shows being spoilt by too much drinking.

Little recognition has been given to the continuity of interest in floriculture throughout the eighteenth century. Apart from the evidence of these gatherings of florists, at their height from 1740 to 1790, nurseries could not have carried their vast stock of cultivars unless there were plenty of customers anxious to grow them. Nor was the growing of flowering plants confined to florists' varieties: the success of the many editions of Philip Miller's famous *Gardener's Dictionary* shows what a wide range of plants were then grown.

The book which stimulated modern interest in florists and their flowers was the delightful *Old Fashioned Flowers* by Sacheverell Sitwell (1939 and 1948). He wrote of 'the florist's art being old enough, even now, to have enjoyed two "Golden Ages"; the first being in the seventeenth century while the second epoch lasted from 1820 to 1870'. It is now clear that there was no eighteenth-century hiatus: all over the country men were meeting and exhibiting their fine flowers at the feasts they held in local inns.

The gardens in which these flowers were grown were formal; even in the eighteenth century such plants had to be kept in easily accessible beds. From various surviving garden plans it is clear, from the way in which numbers are placed on various parts of the plan, that a precise record could be kept of what was planted in each position, possibly changed from year to year. These fine auriculas, carnations and tulips were grown in the gardens of the aristocracy as well as in those of country clergy, doctors, businessmen and tradesmen, but, as the eighteenth century progressed, less in the former and far more in gardens of those of moderate or even humble means.

13 (left). *One of the square beds from the plan of the Reverend Walter Stonehouse's garden at Darfield, Yorkshire, in 1640.*

14 (below). *'The Spring Garden' in 'Hortus Floridus' by Crispin de Passe 1615.*

15. *Frontispiece of the 'Beauties of Flora', showing many of the florists' flowers, by Samuel Curtis, 1820. (Courtesy of the Royal Horticultural Society.)*
16. *Vignette used by the Norfolk and Norwich Horticultural Society in its publications from 1830.*

THE REWARD OF INDUSTRY

NORFOLK and NORWICH HORTICULTURAL SOCIETY

Florists' societies, shows and gardens in the nineteenth century

The nineteenth century saw the flowering of the florist movement amongst people of humble position, a phenomenon notable in, though not confined to, the industrial North and Midlands. Weavers and miners, stocking- and lace-makers met in public houses to show off their tulips, auriculas, pinks and carnations and to weigh their giant gooseberries. As mentioned previously, there was a great reduction in the number of florists' feasts taking place towards the end of the previous century. However, Loudon, writing in 1822, said that the florists' societies so popular in the eighteenth century had 'declined towards the end of last century, but have since revived, and are now rather on the increase', so this late eighteenth-century reversal was only temporary.

Once the popular horticultural journals made their appearance in the 1830s there is much information about the shows that were held. The first of these publications concerned with florists' activities was the *Floricultural Cabinet* founded in 1833, which, with some changes of name, continued until 1916. Later came the *Midland Florist* (1847-63) and the *Florist* (1848-84, which also underwent changes of name), with many good illustrations of florists' flowers. The year 1848 also saw the *Cottage Gardener* make its appearance; this continued as the *Journal of Horticulture* until 1915, while the excellent weekly, the *Gardener's Chronicle*, began publication in 1841. There were many others, some lasting only a few years.

Before these journals appeared most of our information comes from *An Account of Flower Shews held in Lancashire, Cheshire and Yorkshire etc.* which was published annually in the 1820s. It is a valuable source, even though it did not cover all the shows held in the south of the country. In 1826, fifty auricula and polyanthus shows, 27 tulip, nine ranunculus, nineteen pink and 48 carnation shows were reported. Immense amounts of information were provided : for instance, after reporting the names of the winning varieties up to the eighth place for each class at a show, there is an inclusive list of all the plants shown in that class, so, for example, 57 green-edged auriculas and 71 scarlet bizarre carnations are named and placed in order of their winning points.

Prizes at these shows were frequently copper kettles, which continued to be presented for much of the century. In 1860 a gooseberry grower was said to have thirty such kettles hanging from the ceiling of his living room. Public houses would hang out a kettle on the day of a show and a florist, Clough, named his new auricula 'Jingling Johnny', recalling the sound made by the kettles.

The best account of how these societies were organised was given by Thomas Hogg in *A concise and practical Treatise on the Carnation etc* (1822). He gives the rules of two London societies holding auricula, pink and carnation shows. The subscription for each section was 10s 6d and a dinner had to be bought, with fines for non-attendance. After the 1 p.m. dinner, the judges made their decision and then the flowers were passed round, beginning on the president's right. Great care had to be taken that the judges should be ignorant of the ownership of the flowers and, as at the feasts of earlier times, heavy penalties were given to anyone exhibiting a plant which had not been in his possession for at least three months. At this date auriculas and polyanthuses were exhibited in pots and tulips and other flowers in bottles or small vases, though by the 1850s they were shown on cards or boards: the shortened stalks were passed through holes in the board into small water-filled containers. The flowers were 'dressed' for exhibition: errant petals could be removed but insertion of improved ones was not permitted. Hogg gives a good account of the process and tells of a 'frisseur' famous for his skill in dressing flowers.

Around 1830 a wholly new kind of horticultural society appeared on the scene. This development was designed to meet a new kind of need, that of a new race of gardeners: those who were in charge of the sizable gardens attached to the villa homes of industrialists and other well-to-do people, such as were being built in many parts of the country. These gardeners were well trained and skilled in the culture of exotic plants and fine fruits, which they grew in the ever improving greenhouses. Those like Paxton of Chatsworth and McIntosh of Claremont were men of outstanding ability and they set a high standard.

These gardeners required societies where they might meet and shows at which they could exhibit their fine products. Loudon was a key figure at this time as he wrote books for the villa gardener and devised the type of gardening known as 'garden-esque' so suited to them. He also published, from 1826 to 1843, the *Gardener's Magazine* aimed particularly at the professional gardeners whose welfare he defended. The Horticultural Society of London (from 1861 the Royal Horticultural Society) was formed in 1804 but it was only after its first show was held in 1827 that the large provincial horticultural societies were formed in response to the new needs and outlook of the gardening world. A number of the societies formed at this time have survived to celebrate recently their 150th anniversaries.

They all held their shows, usually five annually, at the time when the florists' flowers were in bloom, clearly demonstrating the continuing importance of these plants. A good example of the societies formed at this time is provided by the Norfolk and Norwich Horticultural Society. It was founded in 1829 and is still one of the most successful of the provincial societies, having a membership of about eight hundred and holding four shows each year. (The daffodil, rose, dahlia and chrysanthemum, respectively, are the most important flowers at these shows). Excellent records have survived which show that in the days of the early shows there were classes for all eight of the florists' flowers.

Almost at the same time as this large society was being formed there was a revival in Norwich of a more old-fashioned kind. The *Norwich Chronicle* of 1828 reported that 'an artisan, named Dover, had brought plants with him from the north and west' and that 'about thirty of the Sons of Flora [the name long given to florists in Norwich] had met to hold shows at the Pot-o'-Flowers in the manner known in Lancashire and Yorkshire'. This same Dover won many prizes at the shows of the Norfolk and Norwich Society, while at their tulip show of 1832 more than a thousand blooms were exhibited, most of which had been supplied by 'florists and cottagers'. In the Society's records is an account of the uses made of all those silver spoons won at shows. It was stated that 'many an industrious, skilful man may furnish himself with a set of silver tea spoons ... and eat his peas with a handsome silver dessert spoon instead of a pewter or an iron ladle'.

The close link between florists and the large horticultural societies being formed in the 1830s can also be seen in the early days of the Royal Oxfordshire Horticultural Society. Founded in 1830, this Society is also still in existence and holds three shows each year, one in summer and two in the autumn when the chief plants are the dahlia and chrysanthemum. However, there are classes for vegetables and, as at most societies at the present time, floral art plays an important part at all the shows. Amongst Oxford florists who were active in the formation of the Royal Oxfordshire Horticultural Society were William Collcutt, a waggonmaster and raiser of carnations, and James Maltby, a schoolmaster, one of whose auriculas was illustrated in the *Florist*

in 1853. Professor Daubeny, who became director of the Botanic
Garden in 1834, was a good friend to the Society and allowed it to
hold its summer shows in the garden; these were subsequently
held in various college gardens.

The Ipswich and East of England Horticultural Society, which
has now amalgamated with the Ipswich Gardens' Association,
was formed in 1828 and in its early days held the usual five shows
to coincide with the flowering time of the florists' flowers. Figure
17 is an illustration of the summer show held in 1844. The show
schedules of these societies are usually far too extensive to quote
in full but that of the Aylesbury Floral and Horticultural Society
of 1829 is conveniently brief:

Auriculas, Polyanthuses, Cucumbers and Apples	20 April
Tulips and Anemones	18 May
Ranunculuses, Pinks and Strawberries	29 June
Carnations, Picotees, Melons, Currants,	
Gooseberries and Raspberries	3 August
Apples	5 October

Many societies of those formed around this time foundered:
one such, extremely successful in its day, was the Royal South
London Floricultural Society, which held its major shows at the
Surrey Zoological Society's garden off the Walworth Road.
These shows were attended by vast numbers and it was reported
that at the Society's dahlia show of 1838 over a million blooms
were displayed. The society seems to have failed when the
attractively designed zoological gardens closed in 1856. The
shows organised by these large provincial societies were great
social occasions and remained so until the First World War.

The Annals of Horticulture of 1848 had an article discussing the
two kinds of horticultural societies and saying that there were few
records of the smaller ones since their members could rarely
'write or read writing', but that they 'followed the flower fancy ...
with an earnestness bordering on monomania'. Such earnestness
was nicely shown by the young florist who got up in the middle of
the night to cover his tulips with his blankets when there was a
sudden threat of frost. Meanwhile, the large societies became
ever grander and special classes were set aside for 'cottagers'.
Sensibly, prizes were not offered for anything requiring a heated
greenhouse but, patronisingly, it was hoped that such competitions would help to 'lift them [the cottagers] out of the degrading
habits of sluggish pauperism'. Class distinctions were rigidly
adhered to. In the 1860 membership list of the Horticultural

17. *Ipswich Horticultural Fête, 27th June 1844. (Photograph: Mr E. H. Fisk.)*

Society of London, Joseph Paxton was entered as 'gardener', though he was allowed the privileges of a Fellow (and this when he was already Sir Joseph Paxton MP).

By the mid nineteenth century, when a rail network had been established, national societies were formed for tulips and carnations and gradually the old local associations for special flowers tended to disappear. After an abortive attempt in the 1860s, a national auricula society was formed in 1873 but by then some of the old florists' flowers had ceased to be grown for competition: these included the hyacinth, ranunculus and anemone. Meanwhile, many bedding plants became classified as 'florists' flowers'.

Horticultural journals do not tell us much about the gardens of these artisan florists, since their concern was with cultivation, but there are a few descriptions here or elsewhere. William Howitt in 1844 wrote *Rural Life in England* in which he described a florist's garden in the Hunger Hill allotments of Nottingham. Some of these long-established allotments survive to the present day and are unusual in that each is surrounded by a hedge or fence. Howitt, having described how most of the gardens had a summerhouse and what was grown, writes, 'In another is a florist, with his show of tulips, ranunculuses, hyacinths, carnations, or other choice flowers, that claim all his leisure moments, and are a source of a thousand cares and interests . . . of late, the splendid dahlia and the pansy have become objects of his attention'.

John Hufton, mentioned by Howitt, was a stocking-maker who lived in a cottage on the estate of 'Squire Munday' (after whom one of his finest carnations was named) at Shipley in Derbyshire. Hufton was a noted raiser and winner of many prizes for his polyanthuses, carnations and picotees, some of which were still being sold long after his death. This had occurred some years before an article appeared in the *Midland Florist* of 1851 describing his garden as having an ideal situation: 'facing south and sheltered from the north east by extensive woods'. From these woods he had 'unlimited supplies of that florist's treasure — decaying leaves and also willowdust'. (The latter, the material that collects in old pollarded willows, was something treasured by florists from the seventeenth century onwards.) Hufton, it was related, would walk as far as Nottingham carrying his plants in containers hung from a shoulder yoke. He was self-employed and, to maintain the right for plants of his raising to carry his name, he would never sell the entire stock of any of them. He could do this because 'he was above want'.

Another florist whose cottage stood within sight of the river Thames had his garden described by his grandson in the *Florist* of 1849. It must have been a typical cottage garden with roses and honeysuckle climbing up the cottage walls. However, we are told, his special love was for 'his Bear's Ears, his Polyanthuses, his Tulip Bed, his Carnations and Picotees'. (The writer mentions how inferior were the latter two compared with the kinds grown at the time he was writing.)

The few descriptions of Northern gardens indicate that they could be some distance from the florist's home: one such is that of Tom Mellor, a shoemaker of Ashton-under-Lyne whose obituary appeared in the *Garden* of 1882. His garden was about a mile from his home and there he grew, as well as his florists' flowers, 'the old double white Rocket ... a lovely grey-blue fritillary, a grand lot of Narcissus Horsefieldi, obtained from old John Horsefield himself, and a lot of other old-fashioned plants'. The Reverend F. D. Horner, hearing of Mellor's illness, tried to reach him before his death. It is good to know, even in those days of rigid class distinction, of Horner's concern: elsewhere we learn that Horner (married to a Krupps heiress) had the silk weaver and owner of a beer shop, Robert Lancashire, raiser of the famous auricula 'Lancashire Hero' (figure 29), to stay with him in his fine Yorkshire home.

18. *Joseph Lakin's Oxford garden in 1889, in 'Gardener's Magazine'. (Courtesy of the Royal Horticultural Society.)*

Though the number of dedicated florists decreases towards the end of the nineteenth century, some enthusiasts still existed, scattered through the country. One such was Joseph Lakin, police superintendent at Chipping Norton, who, after his retirement from the force, settled at Cowley, Oxford, and cultivated his garden there until his death in 1895. Lakin came of a long line of Derby florists and continued to be a friend of Thomas Storer of that town, Storer was a distinguished tulip-grower and no less than three of the varieties he raised still flourish today: 'Dr Hardy', 'Lord Stanley' and 'Sam Barlow'. Lakin's garden was described in the *Gardeners' Magazine* of 1889 and is one of the very few florists' gardens to have been illustrated. Lakin raised a number of much praised carnations and grew a choice collection of auriculas as well as some five hundred tulips. He was a vice-chairman of the Royal Oxfordshire Horticultural Society and a founder member of Dodwell's Carnation and Picotee Union, founded in Oxford in 1881.

The nurseries where these nineteenth-century florists' flowers could be bought will be named in the sections dealing with the plants, as will be the many shows held for the different flowers. Undoubtedly the years between 1820 and 1860 saw the artisan florists' movement at its height.

1 Keysers Jewel Hyacinth	9 Brittish King Anemone	17 Merveille du monde Auricula	Almond
2 Diamond D°.	10 Cœlestis Anemone	18 Lady Margarets Anemone	25 Duke of St Albans Auricula
3 Double blossom'd Peach	11 Amaranthus trachee	19 Juliana d°.	26 Turkey ranunculus
4 Single Orange Narcissus	12 Single Junquil	20 Double Junquil	sweetscented
5 Double Endroit Tulip	13 Loves Master Auricula	21 Duke of Beaufort Auricula	27 Double Cuckoo Flower
6 Glory of ye East Auricula	14 Double painted Lady Auricula	22 Lecroep N.ye Tulip	28 Grand Presence Auricula
7 Double Wall Flower	15 Paliurus Christs thorn	23 Beau Regard Tulip	29 Sea Pink
8 Blush red lilly of ye Vally	16 White lilly of ye Vally	24 Dwarf Single Flowering	30 Double flowering

19. *Robert Furber's 'The Flower Garden Display'd, 1734: April' (also in his 'Twelve Months of Flowers'). The hyacinth in the middle of the group is said to be very like the 'King of Great Britain'. The auricula below it, 'Duke of St Albans', is 'strip't carmine on buff'. There are two double auriculas on the bench. (Courtesy of the Royal Horticultural Society.)*

The flowers

.... near the cot
The reed-fence rises round some favourite spot
　Where rich carnations, pinks with purple eyes,
Proud hyacinths, the least some florists prize,
　Tulips tall-stemm'd, and pounced auriculas rise.

(George Crabbe, *The Parish Register.*)

　The plants which came to be regarded as florists' flowers had to have certain qualities. As mentioned previously, they had to be capable of producing seed (giving rise to new kinds) and it was also necessary that they could be propagated vegetatively (to increase the number of any good new sort). The flower had to have a circular outline (florists spurned those they called 'windmill-shaped') and the petals had to have a good texture and be smooth-edged, not fringed or jagged. If the flower were double the floral parts had to lie smoothly. Whether double or single, some variegation in the colour was desired; these colours had to be related to one another in a particular way, though this relationship could change over the years. The plant should of course have healthy foliage and a stem firm enough to support the flower.

　As reported, a majority of the eight flowers came from the Ottoman Empire, where they were already highly developed garden plants (figure 3). The auricula, polyanthus and pink were of European origin. The polyanthus arose in England as a garden

20. *Idealised carnation and picotee, from the 'Gardener and Practical Florist',*
1843. (Courtesy of the Royal Horticultural Society.)

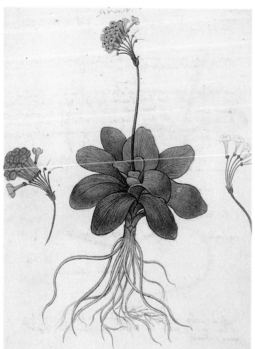

21 (left). *Probably the earliest known coloured illustration of auriculas. From the manuscript of P. A. Michiel of Venice; mid sixteenth century. (Kind permission of the Director of the National Library of St Mark, Venice.)*

22 (opposite). *Fourteen different auriculas from the florilegium of Alexander Marshal; mid seventeenth century. All flowers show some degree of striping. (Windsor Castle, Royal Library. Copyright of Her Majesty the Queen.)*

23 (below). *Florets of auriculas drawn by D. Frankcom, about 1710, for the Badminton florilegium made for Mary, first Duchess of Beaufort. (Kind permission of Her Grace the Duchess of Beaufort.)*

hybrid; as far as is known the only Dutch flower painter to show a gold-laced polyanthus was Jan van Os, and he had close links with England. Of the Turkish plants it is of interest that it was the hyacinth and not the narcissus which was chosen. Both were cultivated in seventeenth-century Ottoman and European gardens and the flower of a daffodil would seem to be closer to the requirements of a florist than the floret of a hyacinth. Possibly there were too many species of narcissus from which to choose.

The flowers are described here in the order in which they appeared at the annual shows, except for the ranunculus which comes before the tulip, not after, since it is usefully compared with the anemone.

The auricula

These brilliant hues are all distinct and clean,
  No kindred tints, no blending streaks between,
This is no shaded, run-off, pin-eyed thing:
  A king of flowers, a flower for England's king.

(George Crabbe, *The Borough*: a florist rejoicing over his prize-winning auricula.)

Of all the florists' flowers none has been so continuously grown and so well loved as the auricula, and rightly so, for, in spite of its modest size and lack of flamboyance, no flower shows such variety and clarity of colour or more elegant form, and to all this it adds a pleasant fragrance.

Nowadays the auricula is divided into a number of groups. The first two, the borders and, possibly, the alpines, are the oldest kinds: the border group generally has a powdering of meal (farina) which is entirely lacking in the alpines; the latter have flowers whose colour shades from dark to paler on the margins. Both lack the special zone of clearly marked meal, the paste, which gives such brilliance to the show group of auriculas. In these, outside the paste is a coloured part which may extend to the margin, in which case it is known as a 'self', or the margin may be formed of a leaf-like area, so giving an 'edged' flower. This edge may be partially or almost wholly covered with meal, giving a grey- or white-edged flower, while if free of meal it is green-edged.

Auriculas first appeared in gardens, probably those of Vienna, around the mid sixteenth century. In the wild they are plants of the high Alps and there is good evidence that they arrived in gardens as a naturally occurring hybrid, *Primula x pubescens,* a cross between the species *P. auricula,* the yellow-flowered, mealy-leaved plant, mainly of calcareous rocks, and *P. rubra* (formerly *P. hirsuta*), the non-mealy, rosy-carmine, white-eyed species found in non-calcareous parts. These species may grow close enough to allow cross-pollination to occur, thus giving rise to the hybrid, *P. x pubescens* Jacquin. This plant was only named at the end of the eighteenth century and from specimens growing in peasants' gardens, but it is believed to be identical to the plant which Clusius, in 1583, illustrated and named *Auricula ursi* II (his *Auricula ursi* I was undoubtedly *P. auricula*). The eminent alpine botanist A. Kerner found all three growing together in the wild and he was the first, in 1875, to suggest the hybrid origin of the garden auricula. The story has been excellently explained by Sir Rowland Biffen in *The Auricula* (1949), where he showed how the remarkable colour range and other features of the plant can be explained by such a hybrid origin. Later writers have suggested that other species of *Primula* may also have made a contribution.

The earliest coloured illustration of the auricula is almost certainly that made for the manuscript of P. A. Michiel (a printed edition of which, *I Cinque Libri di Pianti,* was published in 1940). Michiel was for some years director of the botanic garden in Padua but returned to his home in Venice in 1555, where he died in 1576. The rather odd-shaped yellow-flowered plant with white and carmine varieties (figure 21) had been found in the Friuli alps, north-east of Venice. When in Vienna, Clusius made a special study of alpine plants and his move to Leyden in 1593 must have helped to distribute these as well as other specimens. Certainly, by the end of the century the auricula was being grown in the finer gardens of western Europe. It is most unlikely, however, that Flemish weavers or other refugees coming to England in the 1570s would have brought auriculas with them, as the plant was still a novelty and would not then have had a place in the gardens of humbler folk. In the flower pieces painted at the beginning of the seventeenth century auriculas can be seen only occasionally, as in the wreaths of flowers, where yellow and pink auriculas are just visible. They are not at all conspicuous, as they were to become in later flower pieces or as tulips and carnations already were.

In England, John Gerard was familiar with a few varieties of auriculas in 1597 but by 1629 Parkinson could describe far more,

24. *Portrait of Martha Rodes standing by a pot of auriculas. Signed 'C. Steele, 1750'. Though a green edge is not visible this certainly was an edged flower with the typical four circles. Probably the first illustration of an edged auricula. (Private collection. Supplied by Sothebys by kind permission of the owner.)*

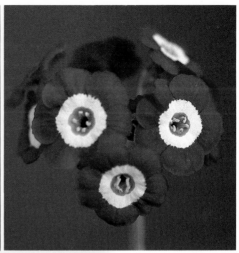

25 (above left). The green-edged auricula 'Fleming-house', raised by J. Stant in 1967. (Photograph: J. J. Wemyss-Cooke.)

26 (above right). The red self auricula 'Docklow Manor', raised by J. J. Wemyss-Cooke in 1984 and photographed by him.

27 (left). The gold-centre alpine auricula 'C. F. Hill', raised by C. A. Hawkes in 1973. (Photograph: J. J. Wemyss-Cooke.)

though he was mistaken in the identity of two that he illustrated. Striped kinds must by then have appeared, as he wrote of the yellow flower 'dasht about the edge only with purple'. A good idea of how these striped flowers appeared is given by figure 22. This comes from an album of watercolours made by Alexander Marshal around the middle of the seventeenth century and now in the Royal Library, Windsor Castle. Marshal died in 1682 at Fulham Palace, the residence of that great gardening bishop, Henry Compton. The flowers Marshal painted could have come from gardens of other members of the Compton family or those of Ham House. These striped auriculas mostly had slightly notched petals and a lightly striped double flower is shown in the top left corner.

Samuel Gilbert was a devoted auricula fancier; it is clear that when he was writing in 1682 there had been a big increase in the number of varieties then available. By then it was striped, and particularly double-striped, kinds which were most admired and could cost up to £20. Dark colours were preferred and he wrote that the only yellow varieties acceptable had to be large and with a good eye, 'the rest not worth a farthing'. Earlier in the century there was a large group of auriculas, known as 'leathercoats', each kind being distinguished by the raiser's name, as in 'Tuggie's leathercoat'.

That eminent gardener, Mary, first Duchess of Beaufort, who cultivated so many newly introduced exotics at Badminton, also grew auriculas, some of which were illustrated in the Badminton florilegium (figure 23). One of these was double, most were striped and one had green tips to the petals; none was named. There is, however, another source for the Duchess's auriculas in the Sloane Herbarium at the British Museum, Natural History. Pressed florets ('pips', as the florists call them) are preserved in little envelopes; almost all are named and are better shaped and larger than those that were painted. Though the colour has faded it is possible to see that some were striped and in many the granules of meal can be seen forming a distinct paste. These auriculas were pressed between 1711 and 1713. Figure 28 shows some pressed auriculas from the *Hortus Siccus* of Jacob Bobart of Oxford of somewhat earlier date. Auriculas continued to be grown at Badminton, for there exists a list of 160 different cultivars grown there in 1746, though by 1761 the list was only of eighteen.

In the Earl of Meath's Irish garden even larger numbers of auriculas were grown in the 1730s, some 230 varieties, including

28. *Auriculas from Bobart's herbarium made at Oxford Botanic Garden. Top, striped flowers; lower left, double flowers. Colour differences are still visible in these flowers preserved in the seventeenth century. (Photograph: the Fielding-Druce Herbarium, Department of Plant Sciences, University of Oxford.)*

home-raised seedlings. Many of the names of these plants, such as 'Duke of St Albans' or 'Glory of England' appeared in the lists from both gardens and were also used of the flowers illustrated in 1730 in Furber's *Twelve Months of Flowers* (figure 19).

Striped flowers continued to be popular but by 1770 the stripes had to be well contrasted and sharply marked off from one another, as Crabbe wrote later: 'all distinct and clean'. Hanbury, writing in 1770, expected 'colours to be as opposite as possible' (also in tulips and carnations). Double-flowered auriculas had by then gone out of fashion, but then, and ever since, primula lovers have agreed with Crabbe's florist in repudiating pin-eyed flowers: in these the stigma protrudes looking like the head of a pin; in the preferred kind, the thrum-eyed, the group of yellow anthers makes a pleasing feature in the centre of the tube. (The two forms assist in cross-pollination.)

For all lovers of auriculas, the most interesting development took place about the middle of the eighteenth century with the appearance of the edged flower. This edging, as Biffen showed, is due to a mutation in which the outer part of the corolla takes on the cell character of the leaf. There are earlier indications of this development in the appearance of green tips in some varieties but it was only now that this feature was seen to add to the beauty of the flower. There has been much speculation about the origin of this new feature. Almost every book or article on the history of the plant mentions the green-edged 'Rule Arbiter', said to have been in production in 1757. This oddly named variety figured in many catalogues of the latter part of the century and was one of a number raised by the northern florist Metcalf. No illustration of it is known but some of Metcalf's other cultivars certainly were edged. A rival claim as the first good edged auricula was made for 'Vice's Green Seedling', known as a prizewinner at florists' feasts in Bristol in the 1770s. Again, no illustration is known but another raised by Vice, called 'Royal Baker' (also a distinctive name), was painted by Thomas Robins the younger, the son of the artist who painted the cover picture of this book (a good truss of auricula is evident in the middle of this bunch of flowers). 'Royal Baker' had a narrow but undoubted green edge forming an even margin to the mauve-purple ground colour.

The lovely portrait of Martha Rodes seen in figure 24 was shown at the 'Glory of the Garden' exhibition at Sothebys, London, in January 1987. It is signed 'C. Steele, 1750'. The large pot contains an undoubted edged auricula, pushing back the date to one earlier than was formerly believed. The names of a number of auriculas which won prizes at eighteenth-century florists' feasts are known and a good many paintings, by Ehret and other flower artists, exist of named varieties, some of which were of fine striped flowers.

By the time James Maddock was laying down the properties required in a good show auricula in the *Florist's Directory* of 1792, many new kinds had appeared, some of which continued to win prizes throughout most of the nineteenth century. One example is the grey-edged 'Privateer' raised by Grimes in 1785 and still successful in 1885. Equally long-lived were some of the finer show varieties of the nineteenth century. One such was 'George Lightbody' (raised in 1857 and still exhibited in 1957) or 'Lancashire Hero', raised by Robert Lancashire of Middleton,

29 (left). *'Lancashire Hero', an edged auricula raised by Robert Lancashire of Middleton, near Manchester, and a long-time prizewinner, in the Florist, 1850. (Courtesy of Mrs Rosemary Verey.)*
30 (right). *The grey-edged auricula 'Warwick' raised by P. G. Ward in 1976 and one of the finest of its group. (Photograph: P. G. Ward.)*

Lancashire, in 1846: of it the Reverend F. D. Horner said 'its body-colour such an intense black, the paste so dense and snowy' and much else besides. By the mid century at least, black was the desired body or ground colour for edged flowers.

The Account of Flower Shews held in 1826 gives a good indication of the large number of varieties by then being grown, for, at the fifty auricula shows held that year, no less than 57 green-edged cultivars were named. Such shows continued to be held mainly, but not exclusively, in industrial areas. In this 1826 description there is reference to another kind of auricula, the alpine, then usually shown as the shaded auricula. The initial interest in this kind had been in Europe, as was made clear in the *Traité de la Culture des Oreilles d'Ours* of 1738 (figure 7), for it was these shaded (*ombrées*) flowers which were cultivated in Flemish and neighbouring towns; the author noted that the

variegated (striped) kinds came from England. This bias continued, for in 1801 F. A. Kannegiesser produced a book with
illustrations of auriculas, one page of which showed 'Luiker [from
Liège] Aurikel', all alpine-type flowers, followed by a page of
'Englische Aurikel', all edged kinds, though the names show
some had been raised in Europe. In England real improvement of
the alpine group took place only from 1860, when first Charles
Turner and then James Douglas began to select improved kinds.
Douglas was the founder of the firm which, for three generations,
until the 1980s, contributed so much to auricula culture.
Gradually the alpine auricula came to be appreciated for its
lovely velvet colouring, graduating from dark to light from its
gold or light centres.

No national society was formed in the mid nineteenth century
for this plant as had been done for the tulip and carnation. An
attempt to found one in the 1860s failed but the tireless Reverend
F. D. Horner succeeded in establishing the National Auricula
Society in 1873. This was followed a few years later by the
southern section formed by James Douglas and others. In the
twentieth century the Society has been renamed the National
Primula and Auricula Society and a Midlands section has been
added. Each section pubishes a Yearbook and holds an annual
primula show for species *Primula* and an auricula show at which
the gold-laced polyanthus is also exhibited. Members visit and
exhibit at each other's shows. Amongst the many classes are some
for border auriculas, the plants closest to those which descended
from the mountains, and also classes for striped and double-
flowered auriculas. Two of the leading raisers of striped kinds are
Allan Hawkes and Gwen Baker; however, we have to thank
American growers for much of the renewed interest in double-
flowered auriculas. Florence Bellis obtained some English seed
and, by careful selection over many years, succeeded in producing some good doubles. An American Primrose Society was
formed and celebrates its jubilee in 1992; it publishes a quarterly
journal, *Primroses.*

Since the 1950s there has been a great revival in growing and
raising auriculas by hybridisation between carefully chosen
parent varieties. There is no doubt that, beautiful as the old
varieties were, modern ones outstrip them in smoothness of
outline, flatness of the flower, proportions of the parts as well as
the splendid array of colours in selfs and alpines. It is impossible
to do justice to the many people who have contributed to this
revival or record more than a very few of the many fine cultivars,

such as the green-edged 'Fleminghouse' (J. Stant 1967) in figure
25, and 'Prague' (D. J. Hadfield 1976); the grey-edged 'Margaret
Martin' (A. J. Martin 1973) and 'Warwick' (P. G. Ward 1976) in
figure 30; the blue self 'Oakes Blue' (D. L. Telford 1974) and the
red self 'Docklow Manor' (J. J. Wemyss-Cooke 1984) in figure
26; and the gold-centre 'C. J. Hill' (C. A. Hawkes 1973) in figure
27. This list does less than justice to those who raised fine
auriculas in the 1950s and 1960s. It is of interest, according to an
entry in *Primroses* (summer 1987) that ever since the eighteenth
century, there has been in Japan a cult of *P. sieboldii* comparable
to the English devotion to the auricula.

The polyanthus

> Or polyanthus, edged with golden wire
> The poor man's flower, that lifts his humble fame
> Till e'en in print appears his envied name.

(Ebenezer Elliott, *Withered Wild-Flowers*, 1840.)

It is generally agreed that the polyanthus arose as a hybrid
between the common primrose, *Primula vulgaris,* and the
cowslip, *P. veris*, though between cultivated, not wild, plants.
The hybrid *P. x variabilis*, the polyanthus, made its appearance in
seventeenth-century England. The special form which became a
florists' flower in the next century was the gold-laced polyanthus.
    When wild primroses and cowslips grow close enough together
a hybrid can arise, known as the false oxlip; this has flowers like
the primrose but they are carried as a group (an umbel) at the top
of a stalk (peduncle), like a cowslip. However, the hybrid of the
seventeenth century had red, not yellow, flowers. No red-
flowered primula seems to have been known to Parkinson when
he wrote the *Paradisus* in 1629, but when his *Theatrum
Botanicum* appeared in 1640 he wrote of 'Tradescants Turkie
purple Primrose' (the reddish-flowered subspecies that is common in Asia Minor). Shortly afterwards Hanmer and Rea
described various red primulas, some of which could well have
been early forms of polyanthus, such as Rea's 'red Cowslips or
Oxlips … some bigger like Oxlips, others smaller like Cowslips'.
The word polyanthus for a distinct kind of primula came into use
in the 1670s (polyanthos was used for a plant with an umbel of
flowers, such as a multi-flora narcissus). William Lucas's catalogue of 1677 offered seeds as well as plants of 'polyanthos all

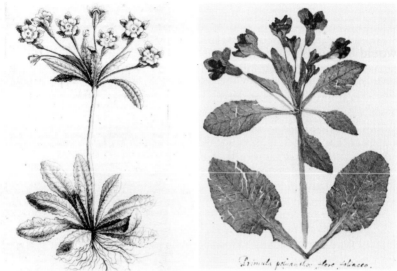

Primula polianthos flore tobacceo.

31 (left). *Believed to be the earliest illustration of a polyanthus. From the catalogue made in 1678 by Paul Hermann at the Botanic Garden of Leyden. (Photograph courtesy of the Director of the Botanic Garden, Leiden, Netherlands.)*

32 (right). *A specimen from Bobart's Oxford herbarium showing the similarity to the Leyden drawing, the plant for which had been sent by Bobart. (Photograph: the Fielding-Druce Herbarium, Department of Plant Sciences, University of Oxford.)*

sorts' and Gilbert, in his book of 1682, wrote of 'the Polianthus's I have' while about the same date '200 poliantheys' were growing at Ham House.

Figure 31 shows what is generally believed to be the earliest illustration of a polyanthus: it comes from the 1687 catalogue of the Botanic Garden at Leyden. The accompanying description states that the drawing was made from a red-flowered plant provided by 'Bobart of Oxford garden'. Jacob Bobart, some of whose auriculas were shown in figure 28, followed his father as keeper of the Oxford physic garden and made a *Hortus Siccus* of plants growing there. Figure 32 shows a specimen from this herbarium. It has all the features of the Leyden drawing: especially noticeable are the tufts of bracts at the base of the umbels in each of these illustrations. Bobart's flowers are too dark to have been yellow. Other sheets of this herbarium have 'cowslips yellow and red' and 'Tradescant's Turkish red primroses'.

In the beautiful florilegium made for the Duchess of Beaufort between 1703 and 1705 is the red-flowered polyanthus shown in figure 41. Apart from the lack of the tuft of bracts, it shows the same features as the Leyden and Oxford specimens. All three would be what is now known as a Jack-in-the-green, with the red corolla nearly hidden by the enlarged green calyx. In a second volume of this florilegium, made a few years later, by a second (and inferior) artist, are drawings of scattered primula florets, some of which show the beginning of lacing and are marked X in figure 33. Lacing, so essential in the florist's polyanthus, consists of a narrow rim of lighter colour which dips into each section of the corolla so that their number almost seems doubled. Lacing can be seen in these otherwise cowslip-like flowers. In a manuscript in the British Library is a report of Bobart sending to Badminton a 'Primula veris limbis argenteis': in other words, a silver-laced primula. Maybe he also sent the red polyanthus.

By the time the polyanthus was accepted by florists, the florets ('pips') had to be larger, flatter and the lacing of even width. The Robins group of flowers forming the cover picture of this book shows a laced polyanthus lying on the table, but its lacing is closer to silver than gold. By the time florists really accepted this flower they required the lacing to be close to the yellow-gold of the eye.

Great strides were made in the improvement of the gold-laced polyanthus (GLP) and, in a guide provided to help judges issued by the Society of Florists at Leicester in the 1780s, it was stated that the polyanthus was more

33. *Examples, marked X, of early forms of laced polyanthus from the florilegium at Badminton House by D. Frankcom, about 1710. (Kind permission of Her Grace the Duchess of Beaufort.)*

advanced than the auricula in reaching a desired standard. The plant was widely shown at florists' feasts, usually at the same time as the auricula. In spite of this high quality, it was never held in as high esteem as the auricula, prizes for it were of less value and nurserymen carried fewer varieties. Such few illustrations as exist of the plant, made towards the end of the eighteenth century, show that the form of the flower changed little in the next fifty or more years. Some of the nineteenth-century cultivars were very long-lived: for instance, 'George IV', raised by the Tamworth florist Buck between 1820 and 1830, was still being shown at the Northern auricula show of 1930, though even before this it was said to be 'nearly as dead as its royal namesake'. Other successful and long-lived varieties were 'Pearson's Alexander', 'Fletcher's Defiance' and 'Burnard's Formosa'. All three were illustrated and of the last named we know that the raiser was 'J. P. Burnard of Formosa Cottage, Holloway'. This cultivar had a dark ground colour, but in others, such as 'George IV', it was red. This distinction still holds good though now the dark colour should be as near black as possible.

With the disappearance of the spring-held shows from the 1860s onwards the GLP lost much of its standing as a show flower but it was saved from the fate of the hyacinth and rununculus by the formation of the National Auricula Society in 1873, at whose shows there were generally classes for the polyanthus. From 1912 the northern section of the Society awarded a cup for the premier plant and, up to the present time, there have only been two years when a name has not appeared on it. Nurseries continued to carry stocks, but of unnamed gold-laced polyanthuses. The few named ones almost disappeared during the Second World War. In 1945 seeds from these were sent to Florence Bellis of Oregon in the United States and she, and also Peter Klein, raised some good strains. These American strains were returned to Britain both as gifts and also when the Barnhaven nursery, established by Florence Bellis, moved to near Kendal, Cumbria. It has been suggested that postwar British varieties had a very restricted genetic make-up but it is now known that a number of northern varieties had survived and were without American input.

Plants exhibited in the 1950s had poor, small flowers and it has only been since the 1970s that plants have been seen which rival their Victorian forebears. Plants are now exhibited with good trusses of flat flowers, up to 1 inch (25 mm) in diameter, often six-, rather than five-cleft, which gives a smoother outline to the flower, with the gold-lacing close to the colour of the eye and

34 (left). *The gold-laced polyanthus 'Burnard's Formosa' from the 'Floricultural Cabinet', 1834. (Courtesy of Mrs Rosemary Verey.)*
35 (right). *Hubert Calvert with his gold-laced polyanthus 'Pennington Gem' in 1976. ('Garden News', 15 May 1976.)*

lastly, with a red or black ground colour without shading.

A number of keen florists have been involved and there has been generous collaboration between them. The many who could be named include John Ollerenshaw, Alan Guest and Leslie Kaye. Since it is of some interest to follow the steps taken in one case of the improvement of the plant, a close look can be taken of the work initiated by Hubert Calvert of Wakefield. Calvert, already a noted grower of florists' tulips, was inspired by the sight of an illustration of 'Burnard's Formosa' to try to restore the plant to its former glory. In the 1960s, from seed recommended for the production of laced forms and ten years' selection of the progeny, he raised 'Pennington Lady', which won a first prize in 1975. Later he combined with Allan Hawkes of Hertfordshire (already mentioned as a raiser of auriculas), who had some good plants from American seed. From crosses between the two strains 'Allanbert Red' was raised and was a prizewinner from 1978 to 1982. Though this cultivar died, others of the strain have survived and their improvement is continuing (figure 42).

The poor survival rate of post-war cultivars has been disappointing, so plants are generally exhibited unnamed, but as strains of the raiser: latterly Kaye's strain has provided many excellent plants. It is hoped that, by healthy cultivation in the garden, rather than as potted greenhouse plants and with careful selection, it may be possible to breed out this tendency for the plant to die after flowering.

There are many other kinds of fine polyanthus, some cultivated in the early days, for William Hanbury wrote in 1770 of having 'more than a thousand of Polyanthus Primrose at once in a blow' and these were of various colours. It was only towards the end of the nineteenth century that Gertrude Jekyll began to select pale-coloured forms, later to be known as 'Munstead bunch primroses'. These have only been replaced in popularity by the larger, brightly coloured types since the end of the Second World War. Of these only the more elegant and traditional, and the lovely Cowichan Strain, owe their development to Florence Bellis.

The hyacinth

> 'I have just learnt to love a hyacinth' [said Catherine Morland to Mr Henry Tilney.] 'And how might you have learnt? By accident or by argument?' 'Your sister taught me ... I saw them the other day in Milsom-street ... I am naturally indifferent about flowers.'

(Jane Austen, *Northanger Abbey.*)

The hyacinth *Hyacinthus orientalis* reached western Europe in the mid sixteenth century from the Ottoman Empire, in whose gardens it was one of the treasured flowering plants. Its long, gently curving sprays figure in Turkish art (figure 3). The species is a native of the eastern Mediterranean. The wild hyacinth is less robust but more graceful than cultivated kinds, with bells of blue or sometimes white and with a wonderful scent. It is known that the Turks collected bulbs from the wild, as in 1583 Sultan Murad III ordered 50,000 to be brought from the mountains to Constantinople.

Hyacinths are said to have been grown in the botanic garden of Padua shortly after its foundation in 1543 and in the Michiel manuscript in Venice there is a coloured illustration of a blue-flowered plant complete with bulb; this is probably the

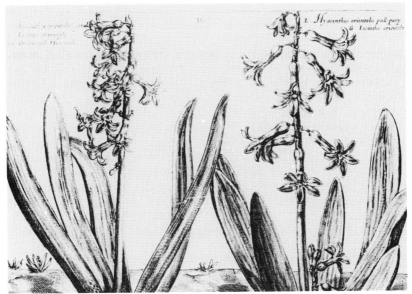

36. *Hyacinths: semi-double flowered on left. From 'Hortus Floridus', Crispin de Passe, 1615.*

earliest coloured representation in western Europe for Michiel died in 1576. He could have obtained the plant when he was in charge of the Padua garden, which he left in 1555. Clusius received bulbs from Constantinople while he was still at the imperial gardens of Vienna and brought some with him when he went to Leyden in 1593. In England, Gerard illustrated a hyacinth plant in his *Herball* of 1597 and wrote that he knew of white- and purple-flowered varieties but they were not in England.

Crispin de Passe illustrated some hyacinths in the *Hortus Floridus* (1615) and wrote of the beauty of the flower 'consisting of three petals, bursting from the middle of the flower'; this was an early semi-double flower, which rare form he said had come from Caccini of Florence. Matteo Caccini was a noted dealer in newly imported plants; he supplied many to the Duke of Sermoneta for his garden at Cisterna, near Rome, and he also sent plants to Clusius, including the lovely tulip which we know as *Tulipa clusiana.*

Parkinson, in his *Paradisus* of 1629, described blue-, white- and purple-flowered hyacinths, some of which were semi-double: he said he had not himself seen 'the full double-white hyacinth'. In the middle of the seventeenth century Alexander Marshal painted a hyacinth inflorescence with five fully double pink florets. (Parkinson had already noted that fully double kinds had fewer florets.) Early flower pieces painted by artists like Jan ('Velvet') Breughel show a few single-flower hyacinths, but they were not at all conspicuous then or even in paintings of the later seventeenth century. Once, however, the true double-flowered varieties were established early in the next century, their presence is very noticeable in the pictures of artists like Jan van Huysum (died 1749). In Robert Furber's *Twelve Months of Flowers* of 1730 both single and double hyacinths can be seen.

Peter Voorhelm, son of the founder of the famous Haarlem firm, is credited with the development, late in the seventeenth century, of the true double-flowered hyacinth. At first he discarded any seedling showing doubling but eventually was struck by the appearance of one which had been overlooked. He was soon impressed by some of its progeny and these double-flowered varieties quickly became popular: so much so, there was fear that something like the tulipomania of a hundred years before might recur. However, though high prices (like £200 for a fine new variety) were charged, this time the mania did not get out of hand.

With the advent of this new double-flowered hyacinth there came a great change in the form of the inflorescence: the long stem with the widely spaced single bells took on a squatter and pyramidal shape, the latter due to the lower florets having longer pedicels. One of the earliest but longest enduring of these double-flowered hyacinths was 'King of Great Britain' (spelt in various ways), the fully double florets having white petals with red inner ones. This contrast between inner and outer petals (so the floret had an eye) was an admired feature. The cover picture of this book shows a large blue-flowered hyacinth of typical form. By 1770 very large numbers of cultivars were available, said by some to number two thousand. In 1777 Weston named 575, grouped according to colour (blue, white, red, purple) and whether single or double; by then some yellow-flowered varieties had been introduced, of which Weston named four. Bulbs were available from English nurserymen but had been imported from the Netherlands.

A little earlier than this James Justice wrote about his visits to the Dutch bulb fields in the *Scots Gardiners Directory* of 1754. He praised the Dutch growers, commenting particularly on the good records they kept so that their varieties were accurately named. Justice was a keen grower of this plant and described 142 named cultivars, saying of another long-lived kind, 'Gloria Mundi', that 'it is one of the finest, largest, and most showy Flowers as yet raised, and at once strikes the Eyes of the Beholder with Wonder and Admiration'. He noted too its well 'reflected' blue petals: this turning backwards of the outer petals helped to give the floret a more rounded outline in the manner desired by florists. As mentioned before, for much of the eighteenth century hyacinth bulbs were more costly than those of tulips but old-established varieties became less expensive and by 1777 'King of Great Britain' sold for 1s 8d. Hyacinths were sometimes shown at the same florists' feasts as were auriculas and polyanthuses; when the Ancient Society of York Florists was formed in 1768 hyacinths were exhibited at its first show, but within a few years the value of the hyacinth prize was reduced relative to those given for the two primulas. According to the *Account of Flower Shews* of 1826, hyacinths were exhibited at most of the spring shows but they were very much third in importance. Some efforts were made to raise new hyacinth varieties in England: one of Maddock's was illustrated by J. Sowerby in *Flora Luxurians* of 1791 and later, in 1835, a collection of 'seedling hyacinths from English roots' was exhibited at Exeter.

While, in the first quarter of the nineteenth century, the florist's tulip was elaborately developed and reached its height as a competition flower, the hyacinth's history was different. Its importance was less for competition than for general decoration of garden and home. Outside it was cultivated in beds devoted to it or in clumps in the flower border, while indoors it was grown in vases shaped so the bulb was supported just above the water. William Cobbett, writing in the *English Gardener* of 1829, referred to the hyacinth's great popularity and was one of those who said that two thousand varieties existed. Giving directions on its culture, he complained of the foolish habit of some English gardeners of discarding the bulbs after flowering. Thomas Hogg, who visited the Dutch bulb felds between Haarlem and Leyden, commented on the hyacinth trade at that time (1835) being larger than that for tulips. There was a considerable export trade to the United States and Russia as well as to Britain.

The appeal of the hyacinth was to all classes. It is the only florists' flower mentioned in Jane Austen's novels: the flowers Catherine saw in Milsom Street probably decorated a shop window. In 1780 Lord Harcourt gave a yellow-flowered hyacinth,

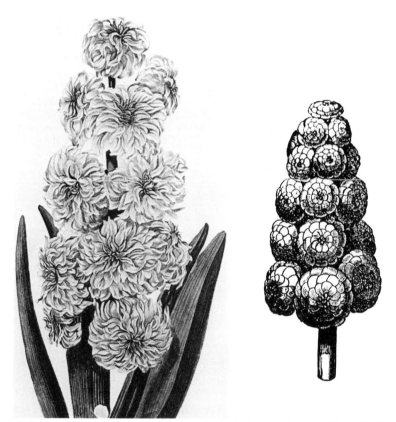

37 (left). *The double yellow hyacinth 'Ophir' from Sweet's 'Florist's Guide',
1827-32. (Courtesy of the Royal Horticultural Society.)*
38 (right). *Idealised hyacinth in the 'Gardener and Practical Florist', 1843.
(Courtesy of the Royal Horticultural Society.)*

called 'Ophir', to Mrs Delany; from it she made one of her tissue
paper mosaics. (Amongst the vast number of flower mosaics that
she made, only the few hyacinths were given cultivar names.)
'Ophir' was a well-known variety, appearing in many catalogues
and being illustrated in Sweet's *Florist's Guide*. It was amongst
the hyacinths that the poet John Clare grew: in his diary of 1825
he wrote of digging up his hyacinths and laying them on a ridge to
dry. (He also grew florists' forms of auriculas and carnations.)
   George Glenny, who succeeded James Maddock as the main
formulator of the 'properties' desirable in florists' flowers wrote
in 1859 that the hyacinth was the least satisfactory of competition

flowers, but he hoped that plants would be produced with 'petals broad, thick, blunt at the end, not pointed, which reflex enough to throw up the centre well.' His demands were aimed at a plant something like the idealised form shown in figure 38. In fact, by the time Glenny was writing, the old pyramidal, double-flowered hyacinth was being replaced by the thickly clustered, domed-shaped inflorescence we know today: illustrations of such, usually single-flowered, hyacinths were already appearing in horticultural journals. We may regret the passing of this elegant and distinctive florists' flower but, apart from a few sad survivors, it has disappeared.

The anemone

> The Anemones likewise, or winde flowers, are so full of variety and so dainty, so pleasant and so delightsome flowers that the sight of them doth enforce an earnest longing desire to be the possessour of some of them at least.

(John Parkinson, *Paradisus*, 1629.)

Two of the many species of the genus *Anemone* underwent the kind of improvement that made them acceptable to florists. One, *A. coronaria,* the poppy anemone, played a larger part than the other, *A. pavonina,* the star anemone. There is some debate about the status of the latter but it is now generally accepted that the brilliant scarlet 'fulgens' is only a variety of it. The pre-Linnaean name for the poppy anemone was *A. tenuifolia* (the narrow-leaved anemone) and for the star anemone *A. latifolia* (the broad-leaved kind). Both species are widespread in the Mediterranean region, particularly in Israel and Greece. The flower colours vary through blue, purple and red with an occasional white form; except for the bright red fulgens form, the star anemone has rather paler colours than has the poppy anemone. In neither species is there distinction into sepals and petals (as is also true of the hyacinth and tulip); both these coloured parts should more correctly be referred to as tepals.

In spite of their distribution in the wild in Europe, anemones seem to have entered Western horticulture from Turkish gardens. The two above, as well as a number of other species of anemone, were known to sixteenth-century botanists and herbalists, but the first person to distinguish between the species and to provide coloured illustrations of them was the Venetian P. A. Michiel (already mentioned in connection with the auricula and hyacinth). The early development of anemones took place in Italy but soon they were being grown in the gardens of the Low Countries. Both self-coloured and striped, red anemones are conspicuous in early Flemish flower pieces, such as those of Jan ('Velvet') Breughel (1573-1621) and A. Bosschaert (the Elder, 1568-1625). Clusius had special beds for them in the Leyden botanic garden, while in the *Historia rariorum* of 1601 he described twenty tenuifolias and eighteen latifolias. Some of his finest had come from Caccini of Florence, who had provided the semi-double hyacinth already referred to. Caccini was also the source of many of the anemones grown in the splendid garden of the Duke of Sermoneta, near Rome. There the finest were grown in pots, but the duke is said to have had 28,000 anemones planted in his parterres. Many of his varieties were given names linking them with his family and estates and were distributed by the Parisian firms of Morin and Robin.

In England anemones were known to John Gerard and in his *Herball* of 1597 he wrote of the great anemone with double flowers known as 'the Anemone of Constantinople'. Parkinson (as the quotation at the head of this section shows) was a great admirer of these plants. Though he gave directions for saving seed, he stated that most new kinds were imported since 'raising seedlings is a great art in the Low Countries'. The anemones illustrated in the seventeenth century have very fanciful forms, as doubling could be effected in a number of ways. In some, both stamens and carpels were modified, the stamens being short, spatula-shaped, coloured structures while the carpels formed a bunch of fine threads, known as plush or, in Europe, as velvet; in others, both parts, or the stamens only, became short, flattened, petal-like structures which could include a few normal stamens, in which case the plant would not be completely sterile, as were the plush kinds. Doubling would seem to have occurred suddenly in predisposed lines.

John Rea and Sir Thomas Hanmer were great admirers of anemones. Hanmer was charmed with the form and the great variety of colour to be seen in his favourite plush anemones. He devoted eight pages of his book to these flowers and to tulips, more than for any other plants. He listed 48 plush varieties obtainable from Morin of Paris, some of which, like the scarlet and pale yellow 'Sermonetta', were clearly linked with the great Italian garden. George Ricketts of Hoxton also provided Hanmer with anemones. In Rea's 1676 edition of *Flora* there is a list of 75

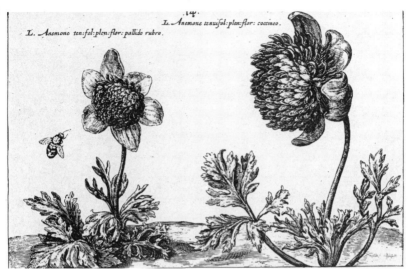

39 (above). *Double-flowered anemones (A. coronaria) from Crispin de Passe's, 'Hortus Floridus', 1615.*

40 (right). *Double-flowered anemones (A. coronaria) from John Edwards's 'British Herbal', 1770. (Courtesy of the Royal Horticultural Society.)*

41 (above left). *Red-flowered polyanthus painted by E. Kickius for the Badminton florilegium between 1703 and 1705. Note the general similarity to figures 31 and 32. (Kind permission of Her Grace the Duchess of Beaufort.)*

42 (above right). *Gold-laced polyanthus raised by Hubert Calvert and photographed by him in 1984.*

43 (left). *Hyacinth 'Koning van Groot Brittanje' from a painting by Georg Ehret for Dr Trew's 'Hortus Nitidissimis'; mid eighteenth century. Note the red inner petals of each floret. (Courtesy of the Royal Horticultural Society.)*

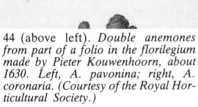

Aurora
133.

44 (above left). *Double anemones from part of a folio in the florilegium made by Pieter Kouwenhoorn, about 1630. Left, A. pavonina; right, A. coronaria. (Courtesy of the Royal Horticultural Society.)*

45 (above right). *Double ranunculus 'Aurora', yellow striped red. Central flower is an example of a proliferous form in which a second flower springs from the centre of the first. From Dr Trew's 'Hortus Nitidissimis'; mid eighteenth century. (Courtesy of the Royal Horticultural Society.)*

46 (right). *Double ranunculus 'Burns the Poet', raised by John Waterston of Paisley, from Sweet's 'Florist's Guide', 1827-32. (Courtesy of the Royal Horticultural Society.)*

tenuifolia and of eight latifolia anemones. Both these authors referred to the Walloons bringing roots from France and Flanders to sell in London. Samuel Gilbert wrote in 1682, of anemones: 'There is a newer Fleece of Flowers, near a hundred sorts of fine varieties of two, three or four colours, strangely placed. About twenty thereof I have in my Garden, many of the rest not yet seen in England'. He also praised those raised in Italy.

When Furber's *Twelve Months of Flowers* appeared in 1730, anemones were still popular: in the illustrations they are second in number to auriculas (figure 19). One of those shown, 'High Admiral', appeared in Gordon's catalogue of about 1770, but by this date fewer of these plants were being grown. Hanbury wrote that they were the least cultivated of all florists' flowers. The cover picture of this book shows a good example of *A. coronaria* (between the hyacinth and the ranunculus on the right side).

John Edwards, a muslin designer by trade, illustrated many florists' flowers in the *British Herbal* of 1770, including the anemone (figure 40). Maddock stated in 1792 that a good flower should measure 2½ inches (6 cm) across and provided an illustration; however, in the two volumes of Sweet's *Florist's Guide* (1827-32) there is not a single picture of an anemone. Nevertheless the horticultural societies formed in the 1830s usually provided a class for this plant at tulip shows and the firm of Luccombe Pince exhibited a 'superb collection' of Dutch anemones at the Exeter show of 1834; these provided a 'great novelty'.

By the mid nineteenth century Carey Tyso was making a great effort to emulate his father's success with the ranunculus (described in the section on this plant) by making the anemone more popular. He wrote many articles in the horticultural journals, particularly a series in the *Gardener's Record* from 1851 to 1853 on the culture of the anemone. The names of the double-flowered anemones that he provided suggest that they were of foreign origin; there would seem to be no evidence that he was raising new varieties himself, as he and his father did of ranunculuses. Possibly influenced by the proximity of Tyso's nursery at Wallingford, the Royal Oxfordshire Horticultural Society offered prizes for anemones between 1856 and 1871.

Later, the species *A. coronaria* made a great recovery as a cut flower. The now single kind, 'de Caen', had its origin back in the mid nineteenth century when Madame Quetel of Caen exhibited splendid specimens and in a catalogue offered five hundred cultivars, then frequently doubles. Later, as the trade in cut flowers developed, her anemones were taken up by nurserymen and the term 'de Caen' was reserved for single-flowered kinds. Then in the 1880s Mrs Lawrenson in Ireland began selecting from a semi-double strain, writing an article about the results using the pseudonym 'St Brigid'; when these semi-double kinds were developed they were distributed under the name 'St Brigid'.

The ranunculus

> And full Renunculus, of glowing red.
>
> (James Thomson, *The Seasons: Spring.*)

The florists' ranunculus and anemone are interestingly contrasted in the stages of their development. Anemones were widely cultivated in the seventeenth century but, by the middle of the next century, their popularity had declined. The ranunculus was much less esteemed in the seventeenth century but, towards the end of the eighteenth, vast numbers of cultivars were available and it continued to be a popular competition flower in Britain until the mid nineteenth century.

The turban or florists' ranunculus is derived from *Ranunculus asiaticus,* a species widely distributed over the eastern Mediterranean region as a single red-flowered form, with a white one common in Crete and a yellow kind in Cyprus. In spite of its distribution, the ranunculus, like the anemone, reached the West from Turkish gardens. There is a tradition that it had been brought back to France by the thirteenth-century crusaders, but, if so, it did not survive as a garden plant. Tournefort, writing of his *Voyage into the Levant* (English version 1718), tells of the Turkish love of the ranunculus and, incidentally, of the importance he held of the Turkish contribution to horticulture, writing, 'Except for pinks and July flowers [carnations] we have no fine flowers but what originally came from the Levant'.

The Asiatic ranunculus was described in sixteenth-century herbals, and even the odd, proliferous form was illustrated in a work of R. Dodoens in 1553. In this peculiar kind one flower grows directly from the first-formed one (figure 45). Such flowers continued to fascinate and to be illustrated in almost every botanical book up to the eighteenth century. They were even used decoratively, as in a glass panel in a window in the Bodleian Library, Oxford, and on a marble mantlepiece of about 1770 in an Oxfordshire house.

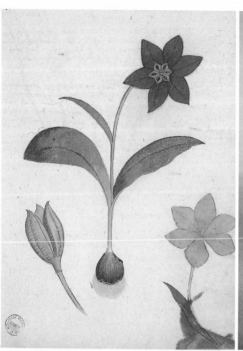

47 (above left). *Red- and yellow-flowered tulips. Probably the first coloured illustration of tulips in the West. A fruit capsule is shown on the left. From the manuscript of P. A. Michiel of Venice; mid sixteenth century. (Photograph by kind permission of the Director of the National Library of St Mark, Venice.)*

48 (above right). *The flamed bizarre tulip 'Sir Joseph Paxton' in one of the stone jars formerly used at Wakefield tulip shows. (Photograph: Mr H. V. Calvert.)*

49 (left). *The feathered rose tulip 'Wakefield', raised by J. Akers. (Photograph: Mr K. N. Eyre.)*

50 (opposite). *Tulips and other flowers from Marshal's florilegium; mid seventeenth century. The tulip upper right is described as 'vis Ray', that is, 'Viceroy', the cultivar which was so popular during tulipomania. Also included are heartsease (V. tricolor), daisies and globe flower. (Windsor Castle, Royal Library. Copyright of Her Majesty the Queen.)*

The ranunculus was being grown in England when Gerard's *Herball* appeared in 1597 and by 1629 Parkinson was familiar with red, yellow and white, even a red- and yellow-striped kind, and both single- and double-flowered forms. The mid seventeenth-century writers, such as Hanmer and Rea, compared this plant unfavourably with the more graceful anemone. However, some idea of its relative popularity is indicated by Alexander Marshal's paintings of about fifty anemones and less than ten ranunculuses: something like the same proportions hold for the illustrations in Furber's *Twelve Months of Flowers* (1730).

When the *Scots Gardiner's Directory* by James Justice appeared in 1754 the position had been reversed. He wrote 'the Persian [dark-flowered] kinds of Ranunculus cannot be equalled by any Flower in Beauty, Diversity of Colour and Form, of these vastly magnificent Flowers' (and this in spite of his love for hyacinths). He recommended the firm of Voorhelm and Van Zompel, whose numerous cultivars, separated into groups by colour, could be purchased for about £4 the hundred. Hanbury commented in 1770 that the red kind was by then regarded as antiquated but he believed should be grown 'by persons of true taste let the fashion for flowers be what it will', indicating that the plant was not just grown for competition. The cover picture of this book shows a ranunculus on the right-hand side and some others faintly displayed.

Indeed, by the 1770s the ranunculus must have been a very popular flower, for Gordon's catalogue of this date offered '649 beautiful, double, Black and Strip'd Persian Ranunculus's' and Weston in 1777 listed 1100 cultivars. The top price was £1 each but most cost much less. The names of these cultivars suggest a European origin, but it would seem that James Maddock, the first to raise tulips from seed, soon did the same for the ranunculus at his nursery at Walworth. In his *Directory* of 1792 he stated that a fine flower should be hemispherical in shape, with well-rounded petals and dark, clear and rich colours, either self-coloured, or striped, spotted, or edged with a contrasting colour. He also said that there were more varieties of ranunculus than of any other plant and that any one kind lasted in perfection only for about twenty-five years, so it was not as long-lived as the tulip or hyacinth. It must have been much grown as a garden plant for otherwise no nurseryman could have carried such large stocks, but it was exhibited at the shows held by the York and Paisley Societies from their earliest days.

Only nine ranunculus shows were reported in the *Account of*

51 (left). *Ranunculuses from John Edwards's 'British Herbal', 1770. (Courtesy of the Royal Horticultural Society.)*
52 (right). *Ranunculuses raised by the Tysos of Wallingford, from the 'Florist', 1851. (Courtesy of Mrs Rosemary Verey.)*

Shews in 1826; three of these were at the not too distant towns of Wallingford, Oxford and Woodstock. The interest there may have been due to the presence at Wallingford of Joseph Tyso (1774-1852) for he had become one of the most successful raisers of this plant from seed since he had settled in the town as Baptist minister in 1819. He wrote articles about the plant for Loudon's *Gardener's Magazine* and later a booklet, selling for 6d. He and his son, Carey (mentioned in the section on anemones), became professional nurserymen and advertised tulips, geraniums, pinks, carnations and dahlias as well as ranunculuses.

Many of Tyso's cultivars were illustrated in journals like the *Florist* and in Sweet's *Florist's Guide* (1827-32), where it is second only to the tulip in the number of varieties illustrated. As well as Tyso, there were many raised by John Waterston of Paisley. He became a member of the Paisley Florist Society in 1812: there are many records of his success with this plant in the pages of the Society's minutes. The *Paisley Advertiser* of 1831 named some of his winning cultivars, including a couple illustrated in Sweet's *Florist's Guide* (figure 46). In the *Floricultural Cabinet* of 1836 a list of about two hundred of his cultivars was provided. Another Scottish raiser of ranunculus varieties was George Lightbody of Selkirk, an all-round florist after whom his friend Richard Headly of Stapleford, Cambridge, named a famous auricula.

All the large horticultural societies formed around 1830 offered prizes for the finest specimens of the ranunculus, but there is evidence that in the 1840s small local shows were held exclusively for this plant, even in towns like York and Oxford where the main societies had classes for the ranunculus at their June shows. Yet, by 1851 Glenny was already writing of it as a neglected plant. Some may have remained faithful to the ranunculus, such as that great supporter of florists' flowers, Sam Barlow of Stakehill, Middleton, who was said in 1880 to have grown two thousand plants. Nevertheless, that other great northern supporter of florists' concerns, the Reverend F. D. Horner, referred to it six years later as 'an extinct flower'.

This turban ranunuculus is still grown from tubers produced in the Netherlands. It is often sold as a cut flower, though mostly in self-coloured forms, lacking the charm of the edged and speckled florists' kinds. However, it should not be too difficult to recover something of the variety and interest of the old kinds if someone were patient and enterprising enough to select from some of the better strains obtainable from bulb specialists.

The tulip

> The Tulip, white, did for complexion seek;
>   And learn'd to interline its cheek:
> Its onion root they then so high did hold,
>   That one was for a Meadow sold.

(Andrew Marvell, *The Mower against Gardens.*)

Of all the Turkish plants introduced, none was of more importance than the tulip. Ogier de Busbecq, ambassador to the Court of the Sultan, described seeing tulips, as well as hyacinths and narcissi, on his first journey to Constantinople in 1554. He sent bulbs and seeds to Vienna and was also responsible for naming the plant in mistaken belief that 'tulipan' (rather than 'lalé') was the Turkish name. Tulips were also arriving in Europe in the course of trade to Venice as well to Vienna. Conrad Gesner saw tulips in flower in a garden in Augsburg in 1559 and described their red petals and the scent which quickly faded. These plants had been grown from seed sent from Constantinople and, because Gesner's illustrated description of them in 1561 was the earliest, Linnaeus named the plant *Tulipa gesneriana*. There is, however, uncertainty as to what species or hybrid this most variable cultivated plant is really related.

In the book which includes all his previous work, *Rariorum Plantarum Historia* (1601), Clusius wrote of the traders of Constantinople offering two kinds of tulips: 'Cafe Lalé' and 'Cavala Lalé'. The second of these, a late-flowering kind, came from the Greek port of Kavalla, while the former, the early-flowering sort, came from Kaffa (Caffa), now known as Feodosyïa, in the Crimea. Of the few species of *Tulipa* that grow in the Crimea there is no doubt that *T. schrenkii* is the one referred to by Clusius. A synonym is *T. suaveolens* whose specific name relates to its being scented. The earliest coloured illustration in Europe of these Turkish tulips is almost certainly that made by P. A. Michiel (figure 47), referred to in the section on auriculas. The red and yellow tulips he grew were referred to as being 'Lalle di Capha in Turchia'. ('Capha' is obviously the same place as Caffa.) In 1630 John Tradescant received a 'Tulippe Caffa' sent from Constantinople by the English ambassador, Sir Peter Wyche. In 1629 Parkinson described and illustrated a 'Tulip of Caffa' (figure 55), though his flower is striped and rather differently shaped. The species, *T. schrenkii*, is scented, with red, yellow, red bordered with yellow, or even white or purple flowers; it is usually short stemmed and is not like the long-stemmed tulip, with its pointed flowers, grown by the Turks.

Almost as soon as the tulip arrived in Europe it began to be subjected to selection and soon many new varieties were being grown; this was all the more remarkable since it takes five or more years before a seedling bulb reaches flowering size. The rapidity with which the tulip was improved and reached popularity is shown by its almost ubiquitous presence in the earliest flower pieces painted by Flemish and Dutch artists. In the paintings of Jan ('Velvet') Breughel and Ambrosius Bosschaert tulips are conspicuous, many-coloured and often show the stripes and markings of a 'broken' flower. This 'breaking' which was so much admired, has been known since the 1930s to be due to an

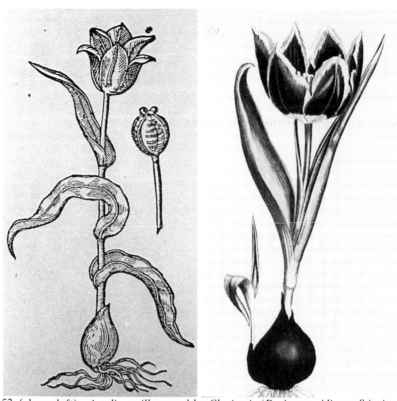

53 (above left). *A tulip as illustrated by Clusius in 'Rariorum Aliquot Stirpium Historia', 1583.*
54 (above right). *Tulipa suaveolens (synonym T. schrenkii) from the 'Botanical Magazine', 1805. (Courtesy of Mrs Rosemary Verey.)*
55 (below). *Number 2 is 'Tulip of Caffa' from John Parkinson's 'Paradisus', 1629.*

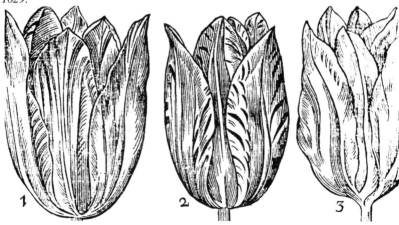

aphid-carried virus. That it was some kind of disease was early suspected: for instance, Parkinson noted that the leaves of broken kinds were a paler green. However, this did not prevent all kinds of devices being suggested to encourage this phenomenon; nor did the presence of the virus seem to reduce the life span of an infected variety.

Tulips were grown in England before the end of the sixteenth century. Gerard wrote in the *Herball* of 1597 of his friend, James Garret, having grown them in his London garden 'these twenty years'. Garret was an apothecary and noted gardener who had been born in Flanders and, though long settled in London, had kept his connections with European botanists like Clusius. Gerard gives some idea of the abundance of tulip cultivars by saying 'to number them were to roule Sisiphus stone or number the sandes'. By the 1630s the Dutch had become embroiled in tulipomania or, as they called it, the 'Wind trade'. Speculation over the sale of new kinds of tulip was completely out of hand and vast sums of money and of goods were exchanged, far more in fact than the 'meadow' suggested by Marvell's mower (see above). Often these purchases were made without any bulbs changing hands. The bubble burst in 1637 and many people were ruined. Two of the most extravagantly priced of all these Dutch varieties were 'Semper Augustus' and 'Viceroy'. The latter, seen in a watercolour by Alexander Marshal (figure 50), appeared in catalogues for a very long time. Tulips and carnations were the first plants to be given cultivar names.

The end of tulipomania was not accompanied by a general decline in the popularity of tulips. However, in the Netherlands the trade became fully professional; it seems that most new varieties were bought by the Dutch from Flanders and France, where they were mostly raised in monasteries. Tulips were widely grown in Western countries in the seventeenth century: for instance, ten thousand bulbs were grown in the Duke of Sermoneta's Italian garden. Samuel Gilbert wrote that his father-in-law, John Rea, had the finest collection in England. Rea had received many from Sir Thomas Hanmer, who in turn had obtained bulbs from France. Hanmer was particularly proud of one he called 'Agat Hanmer', a 'beautiful flower of three colours'. It was amongst the plants that Hanmer gave to John Evelyn. Like Hanmer, Evelyn lavished praise on the tulip, saying it was 'the Queene of all Bulbous Flowers, surpassing all others in richness of colours'. He also noted (a point neglected in most modern kinds but always important to English florists) that the flower should open well as 'the cheife beauty is where the inside is fully seene'. A broken tulip of pale colours can be seen in the cover picture of this book.

Sometime early in the eighteenth century the hyacinth outstripped the tulip in general popularity and soon the old early-flowering tulips introduced in the sixteenth century went out of fashion. Philip Miller wrote in 1759 that these kinds were then so little grown that he could name all the remaining sorts; these included 'Viceroy', 'Duke van Thol' and 'Konings-Kroon' (today's 'Keizerkroon'). The 'Duke van Thol' tulips are also still on the market and closely resemble the species *T. schrenkii*. Hanbury wrote in 1770 in the same vein and declared that the colouring of the stripes must be 'bright, lively and as opposite to nature as possible'. The later-flowering tulips were divided into groups according to the prevailing colour: bybloemens with very dark, almost black colour and roses with markings in shades of red, both with a white ground colour; bizarre flowers had deep red or brown markings on a yellow ground (these being the broken forms which arose quite suddenly from self-coloured breeders).

Tulip shows were held at towns in Suffolk (and, so far as is known, only in Suffolk) at as early a date as 1740, but they were held in York from the establishment of the florists' society there in 1768. In 1775 *Jackson's Oxford Journal* advertised the sale of tulips belonging to the late Dr Tottie of Christ Church, Oxford, which were stated to be the finest collection in England. Maddock's catalogue of the 1770s offered eight hundred late-flowering tulips (and only three early-flowering). The names of most of these eight hundred suggest a Dutch origin; however, Maddock must have begun to raise varieties as one was called 'Walworth' (which was the site of his nursery).

The first half of the nineteenth century saw the extensive development of the English florist or 'fancy' tulip. Large numbers of new kinds were raised, at first mainly by amateur growers in the London area. One of the most noted was William Clark (or Clarke), whose bybloemen 'Fanny Kemble' and bizarre 'Polyphemus' were two of the most famous and long used as parents in crosses. Up to £200 could be paid for a good new variety. John Slater, who wrote so much about the history of the auricula, visited the Dutch bulb fields in 1840 and reported 'the Dutch are a century behind the English ... being only interested in commercial aspects'. Commercially, of course, the Dutch were right, for what could be more quixotic than the English florist's

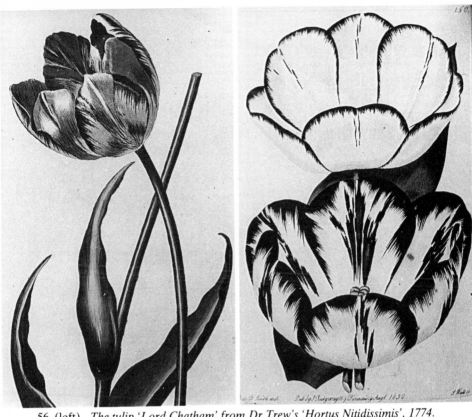

56 (left). *The tulip 'Lord Chatham' from Dr Trew's 'Hortus Nitidissimis', 1774. (Courtesy of the Royal Horticultural Society.)*
57 (right). *The tulip 'Louis XVI', to show feathered (upper) and flamed (lower) markings; Sweet's 'Florist's Guide', 1827-32. (Courtesy of the Royal Horticultural Society.)*

passion for these broken flowers of such a shape and form as to be unattainable in their full glory.

The markings of the contrasting colours could be arranged in two ways: when they took the form of fine lines of colour passing inwards from the edge of each petal and with no more than a fine line of colour up the middle, the flower was said to be feathered; it was flamed when there was a strong central bar up the middle of each petal. A breeder could break into either or both of these forms and offset bulbs from them would breed true. Figure 58 shows the ideal shape, exposing the stamens and pure white or yellow bottom.

In the *Account of Flower Shews* of 1826, 27 tulip shows were reported; these were held mainly in the industrial regions, especially in the Midlands. In 1849 the National (later the Royal National) Tulip Society was formed and this helped to reconcile

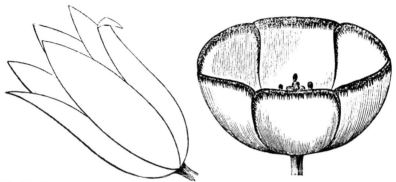

58. *Idealised tulip on right, undesirable form on left; 'Gardener and Practical Florist', 1843. (Courtesy of the Royal Horticultural Society.)*

the differences between northern and southern florists: the former were concerned with the symmetry and beauty of the markings, whilst the latter concentrated on the shape of the flower and the purity of the bottom colour. Undergoing various vicissitudes the Society carried on until 1936 when it handed over its assets to the Wakefield and North of England Tulip Society. The latter had been in existence since 1836 and continues to hold a tulip show in Wakefield each May.

Many of the cultivars still exhibited are now 150 years old or more. In 1973 a descriptive list of the tulips then grown was made by the Society's secretary and this, with some articles by stalwarts of the previous generation, is sent to all new members. Amongst some of the older cultivars still being grown are: the roses 'Juliet' (Willison about 1850), 'Julia Farnese' (Slater about 1850) and 'Mabel' (Martin about 1860); the bybloemens 'Talisman' (Hardy 1860) and 'Bessie' (Hepworth about 1860); the bizarres 'D. Hardy' and 'Sam Barlow' (Storer 1860s) and 'Sir Joseph Paxton' (Willison 1851). 'Sir Joseph Paxton' and 'Sam Barlow' are said to be the most satisfactory of the old cultivars.

Like all good florists, members are not only conservers of old varieties but are concerned to raise new kinds, two of which are the rose 'Wakefield', raised by J. Akers (figure 49) and the bybloemen 'Agbrigg' by H. V. Calvert. Two families which have been closely involved with the welfare of the Wakefield and North of England Tulip Society are the Akers and the Eyres, both now in the third generation, of which the latest are young women. Though there is no longer a commercial source of the bulbs of these beautiful florists' tulips, membership and interest in the Society is now increasing.

The pink

> Tell me where I may have for my monye, all kinds of
> coloured Pynkes, to sett in a Quarter of my Garden or any
> such flowers as perfume the Ayre.

> (Sir Henry Wotton, Provost of Eton College in a letter of the
> 1630s to Thomas Johnson, editor of the improved version of
> Gerard's *Herball* of 1633.)

The pink occupies a peculiar position amongst florists' flowers
for, though it was well loved from Tudor times, it did not until
late in the eighteenth century undergo the kind of improvement
necessary to make it acceptable to florists, and so was the last to
join the eight florists' flowers.

The cultivated pink is derived from *Dianthus plumosus,* though
probably with admixture from other *Dianthus* species. The
species has single flowers ¾ to 1½ inches, (20 to 40 mm) in
diameter with pink or white deeply fringed petals and is sweetly
scented. It flowers June-July and is found in the mountainous
regions of central Europe. Illustrations of the flower are
commonly seen amongst the scattered flowers on the margins of
pages of books of hours (figure 1) and are shown in the top centre
of figure 64, taken from a book of about 1590.

Pinks were grown in English gardens certainly by the sixteenth
century and when Parkinson wrote the *Paradisus* in 1629 he was
familiar with a number of kinds and also with some of our native
species, all of which he lumped together as 'wild or small
gilloflowers'. John Rea, writing in the mid seventeenth century,
considered that pinks 'only serve to set the sides of borders in
spacious gardens, and some for Posies, mixed with the buds of
Damask roses'. Even as late as the 1770s, when James Gordon's
catalogue appeared with long lists of carnations, tulips and other
plants, he named only six pinks ('Pheasant eye', 'Dobson's',
'Painted Lady', 'Clove', 'Old Man's Head' and 'Red'), names
suggestive of groups of similar flowers, as in 'Pheasant eye' for
any pink with a coloured eye. At this date too, Hanbury, who
wrote so fully about florists' or, as he called them, 'prize' flowers,
considered that the pink was not sufficiently improved to be
included and dealt with it in his general section of perennial
plants.

However, by 1792, when James Maddock's *Florist's Directory*
was published, the pink had been accepted. His illustration,

shown in figure 68, is of a double flower with a dark eye and lacing (a line of colour close to the edge of each petal) and with considerable fringing to the petals. Well before this date the related carnation had smooth-edged petals, a condition referred to as 'rose-leaved'. In spite of the persistence of this jagged edge the pink soon became a very popular show flower and pink feasts were being held from the 1780s. Between 1830 and 1860 it was probably the most popular of the original competition flowers.

The story of the early development of the laced pink has been well documented. In the *Floricultural Cabinet* of 1841, the Kent florist Thomas Ibbett wrote about his older neighbour, James Major, who in 1770 raised the first named laced pink, 'the Duchess of Ancaster' (not 'Lancaster', as is sometimes written) and from it raised a number of seedlings, including 'Lady Stoverdale'. These cultivars were still being advertised thirty years later and many florists began raising and growing laced pinks. Later it was found that flowers with fewer petals displayed the eye better and the calyx was not quite so prone to split. It was not until the 1830s that any pink could be said to be rose-leaved.

According to the *Account of Flower Shews* of 1826, there were nineteen pink shows that year, six of which took place in Oxford or neighbouring towns (this area was noted throughout the nineteenth century for its pinks and carnations); one show was held at Chelmsford and the rest in Cheshire, Lancashire and Yorkshire. Flowers were shown in three classes: purple-laced, red-laced and black-and-white. Many varieties were reported as 'Davey's'. Thomas Davey of Chelsea was, at the beginning of the nineteenth century, the leading nurseryman for carnations and pinks; many of the plants he 'let out' had been raised by amateur florists. It was an odd feature about the sale of carnations and pinks that they alone of florists' flowers were sold in pairs. Charles Turner of the Royal Nurseries at Slough followed Davey as the best known nurseryman in the South for the sale of these plants; however, by then the raiser's name was attached to the cultivar name. Some of the finest pinks released by Turner were raised by Dr Allan Maclean of Colchester. A number of these were illustrated in the *Florist* round the middle of the century (figure 59). One, 'John Ball' (figure 60), is still grown and has the distinction of figuring in catalogues or show reports continuously from its first appearance. In 1932 Montagu Allwood used it as one of the parents for a new race of show pinks he was developing.

Much has been written about the laced pinks of Paisley, the

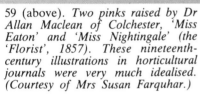

59 (above). *Two pinks raised by Dr Allan Maclean of Colchester, 'Miss Eaton' and 'Miss Nightingale' (the 'Florist', 1857). These nineteenth-century illustrations in horticultural journals were very much idealised. (Courtesy of Mrs Susan Farquhar.)*

60 (top right). *'John Ball', a pink raised by Dr Allan Maclean in the 1850s, the only one of his to survive to the present day.*

61 (second from top). *The pink 'Beauty of Healey', raised by W. Grindrod before 1925.*

62 (third from top). *The very dark laced pink, 'Old Velvet'.*

63 (bottom). *The pink 'Laura Jane', raised by S. Webb of Oxford in 1980 and photographed by him.*

weaving town near Glasgow. It is believed that when the Paisley Florist Society was formed in 1782 members set about improving some of the laced pinks they had obtained from England. The Society's minute books, as well as reports in the *Paisley Advertiser,* confirm that pinks were grown and seedlings raised there well into the nineteenth century. It is strange that we know of no named Paisley pink (against the hundreds of English ones). There is one short list of Scottish pinks supplied by Hogg in his book on the carnation in 1822: of the eleven raisers of these named varieties, four have names similar to some in the list of Society members in 1794. One would like to think that 'Robertson's Gentle Shepherd' and 'Findlayson's Bonnie Lass' had been raised in Paisley, but both these names and those of the other two raisers were very common in Lowland Scotland.

The Society's records make it clear that, certainly between 1810 and 1815, pinks were exhibited over very long periods, from June to October, when, even as far north as this, only seedlings could be expected to be in flower; mature plants would flower into August but not later. It seems probable that most pinks were shown as seedlings, hence the lack of cultivar names (as is now the case with the gold-laced polyanthus). A feature that seems unique to the Paisley Society was the special choice members made in the winter of a particular kind of plant for the coming season. It would seem members were expected to make special efforts to grow the chosen plant.

In 1813 a snuff mull (figure 12) was awarded to Archibald Duncan for the twelve best pinks and the minutes record that the second prize on that occasion went to James Findlayson, a florist of Seedhills, Paisley. Amongst the members in 1794 was a John Findlayson, possibly the father of James, and certainly both were successful exhibitors. In 1806 John sent some pinks to Alexander Wilson of Philadelphia in the United States who wrote back to say that the flowers 'were admired by our American florists'.

In England many pink shows were reported up to, at least, the mid nineteenth century but then in the 1870s came the kind of decline experienced by other florists' flowers. In 1882 Shirley Hibbert advertised in his *Gardener's Magazine* that he planned to hold a national pink show 'to save the plant from its threatened extinction' but he had to abandon the attempt for lack of support. However there were local pink shows and some new varieties were raised; a few have survived to the present day, such as

64. *Various Dianthus from the florilegium made by Adrien Collaert, 1590. The wild pink, D. plumosus, above centre; the wild carnation, D. caryophyllus, below centre. Also various semi-double garden kinds. ('Hortus Belgicus' 1962. Copyright of Bibliothèque Royal Albert 1er, Brussels.)*

65 (left). *Carnations: upper, a bizarre with stripes of two colours, Puxley's 'Jenny Lind'; lower, a flake with stripes of one colour, Mays's 'Justice Shallow', from the 'Florist', 1850. (Courtesy of the Royal Horticultural Society.)*

66 (opposite). *Carnations from Marshal's florilegium, mid seventeenth century. The three flowers are 'Nimphe Royalle', 'appelles' and 'blue Cristal'. (Windsor Castle, Royal Library. Copyright of Her Majesty the Queen.)*

67 (below). *A modern wire-edged picotee, 'Eva Humphries', raised by J. H. Humphries, which received an Award of Merit from the Royal Horticultural Society in 1946. (Photograph: Mr J. Free.)*

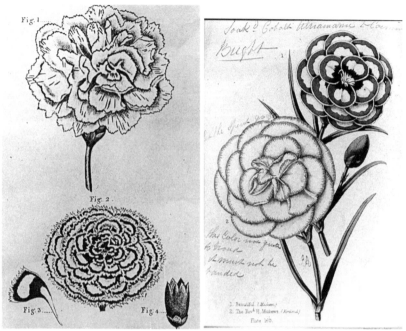

68 (above left). *Picotee (1) and laced pink (2), to show early forms from Maddock's 'Florist's Directory', 1792. (Courtesy of Mrs. Rosemary Verey.)*
69 (above right). *Upper flower, the pink 'Beautiful' raised by Dr Allan Maclean; lower, a picotee raised by G. Kirtland, a shoemaker of Bletchington, Oxfordshire. From the 'Florist', 1860, but photographed from artist's proof. (Courtesy of Mrs Susan Farquhar.)*
70 (below). *Idealised pink: correct petal on right, incorrect on left. From the 'Gardener and Practical Florist', 1843. (Courtesy of the Royal Horticultural Society.)*

'William Brownhill' and 'Beauty of Healey' (figure 61). The latter was raised by W. Grindrod of Healey, near Rochester; a winner of gold-laced polyanthus prizes in the 1920s was of this name and came from the same locality.

Much effort has gone into collecting old Scottish and other pinks, and undoubtedly some have been found. Pinks are hardy and attractive plants and so could well have been kept alive in old gardens but their original names would have been forgotten. When found, they had to be named so we have 'Paisley Gem', 'Dad's Favourite' and 'Murray's Laced'. Claims that laced pinks date from before 1770 can be dismissed, nor is it probable that rose-leaved cultivars originated before 1830.

Of course, there were many pinks which were certainly raised in the nineteenth century, including 'Sam Barlow', 'Paddington' and 'Mrs Sinkins' but these are not florists' laced pinks, attractive as they are. Others are even older. Not only has there been this interest in finding old varieties but also in raising new cultivars. Many fine new kinds are available, both laced and non-laced. It is generally accepted that the old varieties were too show-orientated and that what is now required are more garden-worthy kinds with shorter stems and a longer flowering season than the few weeks enjoyed by the old pinks. The new kinds should, however, retain their charm and fine scent. Pinks are regularly exhibited at the shows held by the British National Carnation Society and at a number of provincial horticultural shows.

There is at present interest in growing and raising pinks and carnations in New Zealand. Dr Keith Hammett of Auckland has raised some 'Kiwi Pinks' and there is a carnation society in South Island.

The carnation

For various colours Tulips most excell,
    And some Anemonies do please as well,
Ranunculus in richest Scarlet shine,
    And Bears-ears may with these in beauty joyne,
But yet if ask and have were in my power,
    Next to the Rose give me the Gilliflower.

(John Rea, *Flora*, 1665.)

Though the species *Dianthus caryophillus* is a native of south and west France, its cultivated form, the carnation, only appeared in western Europe in the second half of the fifteenth century. As Dr John Harvey has shown in *Mediaeval Gardens* (1981) it was first recorded in 1460 at Valencia, having been brought to Spain by the Moors. They were the first to cultivate ornamental gardens in Europe; the carnation they introduced had already undergone improvement in Persian and Ottoman gardens. Soon this plant became popular in other European countries and examples of it appear in the backgrounds of fifteenth- and sixteenth-century paintings, always recognisable as a garden plant by the presence of some kind of supporting frame.

There has been much confusion about the origin of the cultivated members of the genus *Dianthus,* worsened by the vernacular name 'gilliflower', which was also used for some of the scented members of the cabbage family, such as stocks and wallflowers, as well as for carnations and even pinks. The word comes from *gilofre,* which was originally the name for the spice clove (also a member of the carnation family), so when Chaucer wrote of 'clow-gelofre' he was referring to the culinary clove, not to the clove-scented dianthus. There is, furthermore, the problem of separating the carnation from the pink. (Figure 64 shows the two species and also some early cultivated forms.) Undoubtedly some hybridisation has taken place, so it is often difficult to decide whether a plant is a large pink or a small-flowered carnation. In other languages this anxiety is not felt since the same popular word is used for both plants, as in *oeillet* (French), *nelke* (German) and *clavel* (Spanish). English writers of the seventeenth century must have felt this confusion over the word gilliflower since they often changed it to Julyflower, referring to the month it flowered. John Rea, in the second edition of his *Flora* in 1676, made this change in the verse quoted at the head of this section, so that if July was accented as it is now the line would not scan.

Carnations soon underwent intensive selection so that by the end of the sixteenth century there were very many varieties. In 1629, when Parkinson was writing, he described nineteen carnations and 29 gilliflowers (pinks were dealt with separately). He wrote 'I account those that are called Carnations to be greater both for leaf and flower, and gilloflowers for the most part to bee lesser in both'. Colours varied from the deep red of the clove gilliflower to those with white or pale pink petals, spotted or splashed with darker markings. The charm of these seventeenth-century carnations can be seen in florilegia of the period, as in figure 66, from the watercolours made by Alexander Marshal. He

71 (left) .*Carnations growing in a pot and supported by a frame in J. Bock, 'De Stirpium Historia', 1552.*
72 (right). *Picotees. Upper, 'Alfred', raised by E. S. Dodwell, thin-edged; lower, 'Mrs. Norman', thick-edged, from the 'Florist', 1857. (Courtesy of Mrs Susan Farquhar.)*

referred to them as *Cariophillus hortensis* (the usual scientific name of the period) and sometimes as 'Julie flowers'. The majority were also given cultivar names, many of which were similar to those that appeared in Stevenson's poem on the florists' feast at Norwich. This is true for all shown in this plate and for some of the carnations illustrated by Parkinson (figure 6).

John Rea listed many more carnations in the second edition of *Flora,* even more than the 360 he claimed. Though he gave directions for saving seed and growing seedlings, he recognised the difficulty of doing this in the damp British climate. Rea even told his readers how to obtain larger flowers by removing some of the buds.

Carnations were extensively grown in the eighteenth century,

both in the gardens of the aristocracy and by florists who
exhibited them at the feasts being held in public houses all over
the country. In most areas such carnation shows were even more
numerous than those for auriculas. By the mid century florists
were raising their own seedlings for which prizes were offered and
not long after this advertisements indicated that there were by
then two forms of carnations: 'whole blowers' and 'bursters'. The
latter, the older sort, had such a large number of petals that the
calyx tended to burst, producing an untidy flower (as now with
the pink 'Mrs Sinkins'); the other kind, the 'whole blowers', or,
as they were sometimes called, 'French flowers', had fewer petals
and, even if the calyx split, it could be held by various devices.
They had, however, the disadvantage of being smaller. Towards
the end of the century flowers were being produced with a
smooth edge to the petals and because of this were said to be
rose-leaved: 'leaf' was then commonly used also for 'petal'. It is
of interest that Parkinson illustrated one of this kind (figure 6
number 12, 'Master Tuggie his Rose Gilliflower'). There was also
a special kind of carnation called a picotee, an early form of
which is shown in figure 68. It was to be greatly improved and to
become very popular in the nineteenth century. Figure 72 shows
two of these, the very successful 'Alfred', with a narrow darker
edge to the petals, and 'Mrs Norman', with a wider edge.

Apart from the picotee, two other forms of the carnation were
exhibited by the 1770s. These were the flake, which had stripes of
one colour on a white ground, and the bizarre, with stripes of two
or more colours sharply separated from the ground colour: as
Hanbury said of this and other florists' flowers, colours should be
'as opposite as possible'. By the end of the eighteenth century the
carnation was greatly changed from its seventeenth-century
forebears. However, though hundreds, maybe thousands of new
cultivars were to be produced, flakes and bizarres changed little
during their long period of popularity, which lasted into the 1870s
(figure 65).

In the *Account of Flower Shews* of 1826 there were reports of
48 carnation shows; prizes were given for three kinds of flake,
and two each of bizarres and picotees, depending on differences
of colour. The abundance of cultivars that existed is demon-
strated by the fact that 61 scarlet and pink bizarres were named in
these lists of the kinds exhibited that year. Amongst the many
names of those who raised these cultivars is Hufton (whose
garden was mentioned in chapter 3). A great many had come
from Davey's nursery in Chelsea, also noted for pinks. Many of

73. *Carnations exhibited on cards in 1902 in R. P. Brotherston, 'Book of the Carnation', 1904. (Courtesy of Mrs Rosemary Verey.)*

the varieties seen at these shows were illustrated in Sweet's *Florist's Guide* (1827-32) while a variety of other plants was also exhibited: there was often also a competition for the heaviest gooseberries.

The *Midland Florist* of 1850 carried reports of only nine carnation shows; nevertheless, it was in that year that the National Carnation and Picotee Society was established. Like the National Tulip Society, founded the previous year, the plan was to hold a show each year in a different large town, often in conjunction with the local horticultural society. The first was held at the Royal Nurseries at Slough, whose owner, Charles Turner, was a great supporter of the Society, as was also John Keynes of Salisbury (later to be even better known for his dahlias). In the North, the nursery which supported the Society was the Bradshaw Gardens, of Chadderton, near Middleton, Lancashire. This nursery, of which John Holland was the leading partner, was the largest supplier of florists' plants in the north of England. The Society carried on successfully until 1863, when there was a gap until it was re-formed in 1874, largely due to the efforts of the indefatigable Reverend F. D. Horner. (This failure in the 1860s, followed by at least partial recovery in the next decade, also occurred over the holding of national auricula and dahlia shows.) In a review of the renewed show held in 1874, the writer commented on the conservatism of the Society in their refusal to press for garden-worthy plants. He also criticized the custom at shows of displaying the flowers on boards considering that this allowed defects to be hidden and the flowers to be unfairly doctored (figure 73).

A southern section of the society, formed in 1877, worked in close association with the southern branch of the National Auricula Society. Then, in 1881, E. S. Dodwell formed the Carnation and Picotee Union, so called because florists from both north and south could meet to hold shows at his home in Oxford. Amongst the many carnations raised by Dodwell was the picotee 'Alfred' (figure 72). Figure 67 shows a modern picotee.

An article in *La Belgique Horticole* of 1868 described how miners and weavers in the industrial area near Liège cultivated carnations similar to those grown by English artisans; they held the same kind of shows for flowers classified in a similar manner and there was some reciprocal exchange of plants.

By the 1880s the long sway of the flake and bizarre was being challenged by the newer selfs and fancies. These, as well as the older kinds, all belonged to the group known as border carnations, so called because of their essential hardiness. By this time, however, the non-hardy perpetual-flowering carnation had become popular as a show plant and from 1906 had its own society, the British Carnation Society. This soon became the more imporant and, though joint shows were held by the two societies, it was only in 1949 that amalgamation finally took place and the British National Carnation Society was formed. This large society produces a yearbook called *Carnation* and holds shows each year at the Royal Horticultural Society's halls where both kinds of carnation and also pinks are exhibited. In addition, it supports numerous carnation and pink shows held in provincial towns.

Florists' flowers in modern times

In the 1830s additional plants joined the original eight as florists' flowers. First came the pansy, derived largely from the heartsease, *Viola tricolor*, with additions from another native, *V. lutea,* and possibly from *V. altaica*, from Russia. The heartsease, although it had had a place in gardens for so long and had been so lovingly represented in medieval art, remained almost unchanged until the second decade of the nineteenth century when its transformation began in two gardens west of London. The more significant improvement was made by T. Thomson, first as a gardener to Admiral Gambier and later working at his own nursery at Iver in Buckinghamshire. Thomson soon transformed the little heart-shaped flower ('horse-faced', florists called it) into one larger and closer to the circular shape required in a florists' flower; soon too the dark lines leading to the eye (the bee's honey guides) were replaced by a dark blotch (figure 74).

Within a short time heartsease societies were springing up all over the country, particularly in areas where the moister, cooler climate suited the plant. It had the advantage of flowering in its first year and so many cultivars could quickly be raised. This was the Show Pansy, a few varieties of which are still grown. However, around the middle of the nineteenth century its position was superseded by the Fancy Pansy, less rigidly determined in colour and pattern. This kind had its early development in Europe and was first known as the Belgian pansy, but much of its later improvement took place in Scotland. Later still, other kinds of pansy and viola were established as show flowers. Of the many societies formed for these plants in the nineteenth century, a few just survive; their members are dedicated to keeping stocks of older cultivars and of raising worthy new kinds. One who should be mentioned for all he has done for the pansy is Ray Frost of Oakenshaw near Bradford.

The dahlia quickly joined the pansy in penetrating the florist world. Rapid as had been the pansy's progress, that of the dahlia was phenomenal and there was something of a dahlia mania in the 1830s and 1840s. The dahlia is a native of Mexico, from where it was introduced into Spain in 1789, with a second introduction into France and Germany by Von Humboldt in 1804. It is believed that this second supply included plants of hybrid origin for almost immediately new varieties appeared, differing in form and colour and in being double-flowered. The early improvement of the plant took place in France and Germany and it was not until the end of the Napoleonic Wars that dahlias were grown on a large scale in Britain. The development of the dahlia was then explosive and, unlike the pansy, which was mostly cultivated by working-class florists, it was cultivated by all ranks of society. Soon many of the grandest gardens of the land had special areas set aside for the dahlia. Loudon, in 1822, wrote of it being 'the most fashionable flower in the country' and that Lee's nursery at Hammersmith already had two hundred different varieties.

Quickly, too, the dahlia became a show flower; the form then exhibited was the honeycomb, now known as a ball. The *Dahlia Register* of 1836, as well as providing many illustrations, reported 45 shows, some of which took place in the South-west, at towns not otherwise known for florist activity. There were many nurseries specialising in dahlias and offering up to five hundred cultivars. Good prices were paid for the stock of a fine new kind but retail prices were generally lower than for good tulips or hyacinths. In the 1860s, however, came a decline in the popularity of the plant, though recovery took place in the next decade with the introduction of the cactus dahlia.

The chrysanthemum, now probably the supreme show flower, soon joined the dahlia: they became the great autumn competition plants. Though a national society was formed for the chrysanthemum before that for the dahlia, it was later in the nineteenth century that it surpassed the dahlia in popularity as a show flower. As mentioned before, soon after the middle of the century many other plants came to be regarded as florists' flowers and classes for bedding plants and others became a general feature at flower shows.

There has been much discussion as to why interest in growing the original florists' flowers declined after 1860. Contemporary writers, like the Reverend F. D. Horner, laid the blame on the growth of the factory system, together with the great expansion of towns: florists lost their little gardens and even those who did not were no longer able to attend them as they had been when they worked at home as handloom weavers. Others have held that it was the influence of garden writers of the 'natural' school of gardening that led to this deterioration. William Robinson's *English Flower Garden* was published in 1883 and Gertrude Jekyll's books came out even later, by which time the decline had taken place. Though these writers were not friendly towards competitive flower shows, this was because they believed the garden-worthiness of plants was insufficiently stressed at shows. In so far as any dislike was shown for florists' flowers it must be

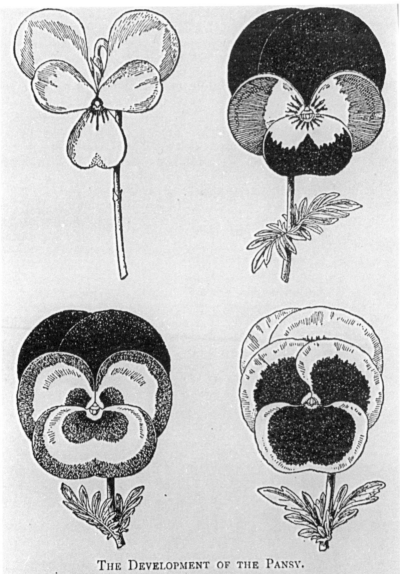

THE DEVELOPMENT OF THE PANSY.

Top flowers (reading from left to right): Wild Pansy and Cultivated Pansy of 1830.
Bottom flowers: Show Pansy of 1870 and Fancy Pansy of 1910.

74. *Development of the Pansy in W. Cuthbertson's 'Pansies, Violas and Violets'
about 1912.*

remembered that by then bedding plants were so regarded. Miss Jekyll was particularly fond of auriculas. Both Robinson and Jekyll and other writers of their outlook stressed their admiration for cottagers' gardens. Their books were not, however, written for cottagers, rather for the owners of larger gardens whom they encouraged to emulate the simplicity and good taste shown in the cottage garden.

Examination of local newspapers and of horticultural journals of the late part of the nineteenth century does not show so much a decrease in the number of horticultural shows as a change in the kind of plants exhibited. The *Middleton Albion* of 1872 provides some interesting information. Middleton, near Manchester, is something of a shrine for florists because it was for so long a centre of their activity. That year the first show was that for auriculas and is of note because it led to the formation of the National Auricula Society the following year. Then came a pink show held in the home of Robert Lancashire, raiser of the famous auricula 'Lancashire Hero' (figure 29). This was followed by a gooseberry show. The remaining seven shows reported were of a more general kind, even if one was called an onion, and another, a celery, show. Prizes of copper kettles, rocking chairs and pairs of blankets were offered for various collections of vegetables and of flowers.

Even more is revealed by the *Gardener's Magazine* of 1895, in which some 150 shows were reported. Of these, no less than 51 were for the chrysanthemum (and dahlia), with only a very few serving the rose, the carnation and pink, or the pansy. The other shows were held by horticultural societies, both large and small, and were of a general nature. For these societies spring and early summer shows were things of the past. It seems clear that the older kinds of florists' flowers ceased to be show flowers largely because members of societies turned from growing them to the culture of chrysanthemums and dahlias or had become more interested in growing vegetables. With no local show at which to exhibit their auriculas and other old flowers, they simply stopped growing them. For the keen florist it is not just the hope of winning a prize that makes the show important; it is as much the opportunity to exchange plants and ideas.

The pattern for many horticultural societies at present is to hold two autumn shows at which dahlias and chrysanthemums are the most important exhibits, and often one in the summer for the rose and/or sweet peas. At all the shows prizes are offered for vegetables and pot plants and there is much support from exhibitors in floral art classes. Of course, there are many variations on this pattern, especially at village flower shows, and there are also other reasons for the changes that have taken place in the kind of flower shows held.

It is salutary for florists to consider from time to time the strangeness of their so man-made, if so beautiful, flowers. There has always been some satire aimed at the peculiarities of their flowers and their habits, such as that in the *Tatler* of 1710. Here the writer is supposed to overhear men talking about kings and generals, such as 'The King of Sweden', 'Alexander the Great' and 'General Villars'. Discovering at last that these names refer to varieties of tulips, he goes with the men to see their tulip beds and disgraces himself by admiring all the wrong flowers. In the caricature on page 2 the entomologist with his net is trampling over the horrified florist's tulips. Among many examples of such satire there is Mary Mitford's account of the farmer's wife (in *Our Village*) who was ' ... a real, genuine florist: valued pinks, tulips, and auriculas for certain qualities of shape and colour, with which beauty has nothing to do: preferred black ranunculuses ... Of all the odd fashions, that of the dark, gloomy, dingy flowers appears to me the oddest. Your true connoisseurs now shall prefer a deep puce hollyhock to the gay pink blossoms which cluster round that splendid plant like a pyramid of roses.' Your 'true florist' is not to be deflected by such mirth from his intention of producing still more splendid flowers, nor is he unaware of the necessity of preserving the finer of old cultivars.

So aware have gardeners in general become of the need to preserve old garden plants that a society has been formed with this as one of its aims. It is the National Council for the Conservation of Plants and Gardens (whose address is given at the end of this book). With the inflation of modern times nurseries can no longer afford to carry the vast selection of plants that was formerly possible, so the society is establishing national collections of plants, both species and cultivars, at various localities throughout the country: in privately owned gardens, nurseries or botanic gardens, or those of the National Trust. Micropropagation has already been used for some plants, including auriculas. It may prove a useful method in maintaining stocks of old plants.

Further reading

Blunt, Wilfrid. *Tulips and Tulipomania*. Basilisk Press, 1977. Fine illustrations by Rory McEwen.
Cottesloe, Gloria, and Hunt, Doris. *The Duchess of Beaufort's Flowers*. Webb and Bower, 1983.
Duthie, Ruth. Articles in *Garden History* (1982 and 1984), *York Historian* (1980) and in some yearbooks of the societies.
Fisher, John. *Mr. Marshal's Flower Album*. Gollancz, 1985.
Genders, Roy. *Collecting Antique Plants*. Pelham Books, 1971. Also other books on individual plants.
Harvey, John. *Early Gardening Catalogues*. Phillimore, 1972.
Harvey, John. *Early Nurserymen*. Phillimore, 1974.
Leith-Ross, Prudence. *The John Tradescants*. Peter Owen, 1984.
Moreton, C. Oscar. *The Auricula*. Ariel Press, 1964. Fine illustrations by Rory McEwen.
Moreton, C. Oscar. *Old Carnations and Pinks*. Ariel Press, 1955. Fine illustrations by Rory McEwen.
Sitwell, Sacheverell. *Old Fashioned Flowers*. Country Life, 1939 and 1948. The foundation work on the subject of florists' flowers.
Wemyss-Cooke, J. J. *Primulas Old and New*. David and Charles, 1986.

Present-day florists' societies and specialist nurseries

For those interested in growing these plants and learning about culture methods the best thing is to join the relevant society. Members are helpful to newcomers. Some of the plants, like the tulips, can only be obtained through the societies. New members are advised how best these old cultivars can be preserved. Useful handbooks are available from the societies, such as *Florists' Auriculas and Gold-Lace Polyanthus* by Frank Jacques (National Auricula and Primrose Society) and *How to Grow Border Carnations* and *How to Grow Pinks* (British National Carnation Society).

British National Carnation Society (BNCS): Mrs P. E. Dimond, 3 Canberra Close, Hornchurch, Essex RM12 5TR.
Garden History Society: Mrs J. Hook, PO Box 27, Haslemere, Surrey GU27 3DR.

National Auricula and Primula Society (NAPS): (Northern) D. G. Hadfield, 146 Queens Road, Cheadle Hulme, Cheshire SK8 5HY; (Southern) L. E. Wigley, 67 Warnham Court Road, Carshalton Beeches, Surrey; (West and Midland) B. Goalby, 99 Somerfield Road, Bloxwich, Walsall, West Midlands.

National Council for the Conservation of Plants and Gardens (NCCPG): c/o Royal Horticultural Society Garden, Wisley, Surrey GU23 6QB.

North of England Pansy and Viola Society: B. Atack, 46 Westgate, Cleckheaton, Yorkshire.

Wakefield and North of England Tulip Society: K. N. Eyre, 67 Beverley Road, South Cave, Brough, North Humberside HU15 2BB.

The American Primrose Society: B. Skidmore, 6730 West Mercerway, Mercer Island, WA 98040, USA.

The Hardy Plant Society: Mrs Sambrooke, 214 Roxley Lane, West Ewell, Surrey KT17 9EU.

Only some of the smaller specialist nurseries are given. It is advisable to enclose a stamped addressed envelope when writing.

Cravens Nursery, 1 Foulds Terrace, Bingley, West Yorks BD16 4LZ. Auriculas and primulas and also border pinks.

Susan Farquhar, Old Inn Cottage, Piddington, Bicester, Oxford-shire. Old pinks. For times of opening see *Gardens of England and Wales* (National Gardens Scheme yellow book).

Ruth and Tom Gillies, 22 Chetwyn Avenue, Bromley Cross, Bolton, Lancashire BL7 9BN. Pinks and carnations.

Hazeldene Nursery, Dean Street, East Farleigh, Maidstone, Kent. Pansies and violas.

Sophie Hughes, Kingstone Cottage, Weston under Penyard, Ross-on-Wye, Herefordshire. Old pinks.

Brenda Hyatt, 1 Toddington Crescent, Bluebell Hill, near Chatham, Kent ME5 9QT. Auriculas and polyanthus, plants and seeds.

Some gardens to visit

Gardens marked with an asterisk have some areas of formal design in which are growing plants introduced to Britain before the end of the seventeenth century. The others are of interest for their design or historic connections. For other gardens to visit consult *Gardens of England and Wales* published by the National Gardens Scheme (the yellow book) and *Historic Houses, Castles and Gardens open to the Public*, both published annually. Intending visitors are advised to ascertain dates and times of opening before making a special journey.

Canons Ashby House, near Daventry, Northampton NN11 65D. Telephone: 0327 860044 (NT).

Cranborne Manor Gardens, Cranborne, Dorset. Telephone: 07254 248.*

Ham House, Richmond, Surrey TW10 7RS. Telephone: 01-940 1950 (NT).

Hampton Court Palace, Hampton Court, London. Telephone: 01-977 8441 (EH).

Harlow Car Gardens, Harrogate, North Yorkshire. Telephone: 0423 65418. Includes a newly-made garden of historic plants.*

Hatfield House, Hatfield, Hertfordshire. Telephone: 07072 62823 or 65159.*

Kew Palace (The Queen's Garden), Royal Botanic Gardens, Kew, Richmond, Surrey. Telephone: 01-940 1171.*

Kirby Hall, near Corby, Northamptonshire. Telephone: 0533 663230 (EH).

Levens Hall, near Kendal, Cumbria. Telephone: 05395 60321.

Pallant House, Chichester, West Sussex. A town garden of eighteenth-century design and planting.

Powis Castle, Welshpool, Powys. Telephone: 0938 4336 (NT).

Tradescant Trust, Museum of Garden History, Lambeth, London (at the gates of Lambeth Palace). Telephone: 01-261 1891.*

Tudor House Museum, Bugle Street, Southampton, Hampshire. Telephone: 0703 24216.*

Westbury Court Garden, Westbury-on-Severn, Gloucestershire. Telephone: 045276 461 (NT).*

Index

Page numbers in italic refer to illustrations; those in bold refer to the main account of that flower.